COMBAT TO CATWALK

KATRINA HODGE

WITH ALEXANDRA HEMINSLEY

COMBAT TO CATWALK

THE AMAZING STORY OF THE GIRL WHO WENT FROM ARMY HERO TO MISS ENGLAND

JOHN BLAKE

Published by John Blake Publishing Ltd,
3 Bramber Court, 2 Bramber Road,
London W14 9PB, England

www.johnblakepublishing.co.uk

www.facebook.com/Johnblakepub facebook
twitter.com/johnblakepub twitter

First published in hardback in 2011

ISBN: 978-1-84358-337-0

British Library Cataloguing-in-Publication Data:

A catalogue record for this book is available from the British Library.

Design by www.envydesign.co.uk

Printed in Great Britain by CPI Mackays, Chatham, ME5 8TD

1 3 5 7 9 10 8 6 4 2

Papers used by John Blake Publishing are natural, recyclable products made
from wood grown in sustainable forests. The manufacturing processes conform to
the environmental regulations of the country of origin.

Every attempt has been made to contact the relevant copyright-holders, but some
were unobtainable. We would be grateful if the appropriate people could contact us.

CONTENTS

PROLOGUE   VII

Chapter One: CHILDHOOD   1

Chapter Two: THE ARMY   19

Chapter Three: IRAQ TOUR   53

Chapter Four: HOME AGAIN – ENGLAND   83
AND MISS ENGLAND

Chapter Five: MEETING THE PRESS   101

Chapter Six: THE SEMI-FINALS   129

Chapter Seven: A SECOND CHANCE –   149
MISS ENGLAND 2009

Chapter Eight: MISS ENGLAND, AT LAST!   177

Chapter Nine: MISS WORLD   205

Chapter Ten: MY AMAZING YEAR   225

PROLOGUE

EVERYONE dreams about the day when their life will change: I know I did – I just wish I'd been wearing something a bit more glamorous when it arrived. As it was, I was in a pair of tights and an old T-shirt, with half my hair straightened and one eye made up. It was just an ordinary Friday night at my mum's house. I simply wasn't expecting the attention.

I was upstairs with the girls getting ready for a night out. It was always the same when my old mates Hayley and Leonie came over: trying on outfits, passing the hair straighteners, fiddling with accessories. While we were up there, giggling and chatting, I heard the doorbell go. I wasn't expecting anyone so I ignored it – after all, I had to consider the important matter of how to walk in Hayley's platform wedges after a month or so in combat boots. The next thing I knew, Mum was calling me from the stairs.

'Kat, could you come down here, please? We've got a lady here who would like to talk to you.' Mum's voice sounded tight, and a little more high-pitched than usual. She was using the tone I normally only heard if someone was rude to her in a supermarket.

'Seems a bit weird,' I thought to myself, 'a stranger turning up at our house on a Friday night'. I don't have the kind of job where you leave the office like clockwork at the end of the day or week and head out with your mates to your local favourite. I'm a soldier, so leave is a treasured time to take off the combats and get out the mascara. I was seriously looking forward to this night out and wasn't at all keen on the idea of an interruption from a random visitor. Catching up with the girls after what had been a while was my main priority. I'm not much of a big clubbing girl, but I just wanted to do my hair, put on my lipgloss and get dancing.

'She says she's from the Sun newspaper,' my mum continued. I could hear her coming up the stairs. Even her footsteps were starting to sound a bit nervous. Hayley turned the stereo down in my bedroom and mouthed, 'What on earth?' at Leonie and me.

Because this was a weird situation, to say the very least: what did the Sun want to talk to me for? And how had they found out where I lived? I rushed downstairs, pulling my baggy T-shirt down as far as I could and smoothing my hair down as I walked. Just like Mum, I was trying not to show it, but by now, there were a few butterflies in my stomach as well. What was going on? Was it some kind of emergency? A friend in trouble and a journo fishing for scandal? Or had I been mistaken for someone else? I had been interviewed for work once before, but it certainly didn't involve a night-time visit from a nameless reporter. This was the stuff of movies.

I was a bit disappointed when I got to the door: the lady looked perfectly normal. Where was her raincoat, her notepad full of scribbles, her sneaky Dictaphone? Instead, she was a perfectly nice-looking thirty-something, with neat, bobbed brown hair, a standard pair of jeans and a leather jacket. She reminded me more of a GAP advertisement than a hack. Plus, she was looking me straight in the eye as I came downstairs, with none of the shiftiness that I would have expected from a door-stepping tabloid journalist. With horror, it crossed my mind that Mum had misheard her and there was about to be a terrible misunderstanding. I took a deep breath and said hello.

'I hope you don't mind me coming to find you,' said the journalist politely. 'But I think you've got a great story, what with your combining serving in the Army with going for Miss England.' She went on to explain that she had seen my photograph in the local newspaper, the *Kent & Sussex Courier*, and had contacted them to find out where I lived. They had told her the name of my street, but left it at that. So she had knocked at every door along the street where I live.

Of course she found me in no time: I'd grown up on that street, and I'd lived there forever. My childhood had been spent riding my bike up and down it and offering to do odd jobs for all the neighbours. But it seemed incredible that I could be that much of a story. In the house with my mum and my mates I felt like the most ordinary girl in the world. Just Kat. It turns out there aren't that many prospective beauty queens who have also served in Iraq, though. For the *Sun* it was a story, for me it was a way of life. And as I looked the reporter in the eye, I knew I would never be 'just Kat' again.

CHAPTER ONE

CHILDHOOD

UP A TREE – well, up a tree in a dress, that's where you would have been most likely to find me when I was little. I suppose I had the kind of childhood that lots of kids today don't get to enjoy – I spent hours and hours playing in the street and woods, and my parents never had to worry about me staying close to the house. I lived in the same house, in Goudhurst on the outskirts of Tunbridge Wells, for my whole childhood – my parents are divorced but my mum still lives there now. But it wasn't very likely you'd find me indoors. I was always outside, you see, mucking about with a bunch of other kids.

I was lucky enough to live on a street where there were loads of children my age. My brother Byran is two years older than me and I hardly remember seeing him as he always had his own gang of friends. It was as if we had divided the house and garden into two: he got the TV and computer, and I got the garden and street. My entire world was outside and I would start to get restless if indoors for too long, while he could spend hours on end playing computer games, or inventing them.

The number of outdoor games I used to make up with my gang was never-ending. There was a big field at one end of the street and we'd gather there, with me as a sort of ringleader among the kids our age – I was around seven or eight at the time. It started off with a couple of girls, then a set of boy triplets joined in, and before long other kids would be added to the group. Our age, new to the street, bored of watching telly? Join us! Finding new recruits was easy: our games were fun and they usually involved some kind of dare or dramatic performance, so curious newcomers always got stuck in before too long.

We put together a football team and would play against kids from other nearby streets. We'd ride bikes, zoom around on roller-skates and sometimes I even used to jump on the horse in the field, totally bareback. From the age of eight or nine, I was totally fearless: I'd just grab onto the poor creature's mane and gallop away, hoping for the best. I don't remember ever doubting I'd survive these escapades. Who cares about the saddle? What was a horse for, if not for riding?

My first heroes were the Power Rangers. Once I had convinced everyone that I had to be either the pink or the yellow one, I was happy to high kick and spin around for hours on end. I adored pretending I could fight, that I had superpowers and there was no challenge too great for Kat! That slowly turned into my obsession with the Spice Girls. Well, what can I say? It *was* the 1990s! I loved Geri's wacky antics but it was Mel C, aka Sporty Spice, who became my real inspiration. I really did love high kicks in those days.

My gang used to challenge each other to climb the trees in the nearby field, just to test each other out. 'Oh, go on, I bet you can't make it to the top of that one,' was one of the most exciting things I could possibly imagine hearing in those days and the phrase most likely to make me want to take the tree on. I loved the challenge. Once up there, we would sit and chat for hours... and only then realise that we had to get back down again.

My instinct would be to prove that I could get to the top of the tree – it didn't matter about anything else. I ran headlong at the dare, didn't consider the risks, reckoning I'd just sort out the getting down bit later on. But of course that meant I kept getting stuck. One day I had my eye on one of the bigger trees: I decided it was time to take it on, and that was that. I can clearly remember climbing up it – I was pretty quick and nimble. The grass below was getting further and further away, and I could tell the other kids were impressed. There was only one problem: as I was climbing, I could hear the branches that I had been relying on to get me up were snapping away as I used them to get higher and higher. Before long, I was at the top. Yay, I had done it! But there were no branches to get down with. I was an eight-year-old in a party frock, stuck at the top of a tree. Dressed to party, but... well... stuck.

It was the first time that my dad had to call the Fire Brigade to get me down. In the past he had been able to come and help me, but this time it was beyond even him. As I sat there on my perch, waiting for the fireman to reach me, I knew I was in big trouble. Dad was going ballistic. I was grounded – literally – for a long time. I think my dad tried to ground me for a month, but it didn't really work – I used to offer to walk the dog as an excuse to get out of the house! They weren't particularly controlling parents most of the time, but I think my dad wanted to teach me a lesson that there were some limits to what I could do. I wasn't naughty or malicious, but perhaps a little too wild: I had to learn that however great my taste for adventure, I had to at least try and take into the account the consequences, or I'd be heading for a fall – from a tree or otherwise.

As you can imagine, being in the Brownies was a little tame for me; what I really wanted was to join the Scouts – they had much better activities. It didn't seem fair that the Brownies had to do sewing and ironing for badges, but if you were in Cubs or Scouts, you were allowed to go camping and do gardening and all sorts of outdoorsy stuff. That was all I wanted to do. The problem was, they wouldn't let you join if you were a girl. It seemed I was stuck with Brownies from the age of seven to ten, but in the end I managed to find a way around it. My brother was in the Scouts and Dad helped out with them, so I would sometimes tag along, pretending that I was keeping him company. Actually, I wanted in on the good activities. Camping and building bonfires at last! Girl Power! Eventually my parents seemed to notice what I was up to and I was allowed to join the Sea Cadets. That was my first taste of Forces life.

On the whole, Mum and Dad were always very relaxed about me. It was just the clothes that my mum used to go nuts about. When I was little, she would try and put me in dresses, especially on Sundays before Sunday school. But I'd always sneak out for a quick bike ride or to check that I could get to the top of a tree I'd spotted, and before long I would turn up at the house ready for church with my cute pastel dress covered in mud. At first Mum tried so hard to make me look girly and respectable – I was her only daughter and I suppose she wanted me to be as pretty and feminine as possible. But after a few years of ruined party dresses and hundreds of loads of washing, she gave up. The Power Rangers and the Spice Girls had won: it was Adidas tracksuit bottoms and T-shirts for me. I didn't really want to dress as a boy, but I just felt as if I had so many activities to get through every day that frills and sashes were holding me back; I wanted baggy, comfortable clothes for my exploits. If only I'd known then what I'd be wearing to work in the years to come, I would have been thrilled. No one can say that an Army uniform is feminine, but it's certainly practical when you need to climb something in a hurry!

As soon as my poor mum stopped nagging me about looking nice all the time, I realised that perhaps I missed dresses after all. Maybe it was just the liberation of not being told off any more, maybe it was just a phase that I would have grown out of anyway or maybe it was the fact that boys were starting to appear on my radar. But after a while I found myself taking more pride in my appearance. I didn't want to choose between being a tomboy or a girly girl. Why should I have to compromise? So what if I was going to spend my day up a tree, rolling around in mud, or bashing boys with sticks? I was going to do it in a decent outfit. I would prove to the new kid on the street that the girl with the long hair could still shin it up a tree as fast as him. And I'd make sure the local girls knew I took care of my appearance, even if I spent more time outside than admiring the All Saints on MTV.

As much as I liked doing all of the tomboy stuff, there was another part of my childhood that was really important to me: performing. Our gang of kids used to take great pride in putting on shows for the younger kids on the street. I'd persuade my group to be in my band with me as lead singer and we'd put on shows for the entire street, all dressed up. The details of the show would change – Christmas spectaculars, Easter shows, summer concerts – but some things would remain the same. We would rehearse for hours: organising the running order, polishing our performances, selecting the costumes. Then we'd either set out chairs in the garden or line up the parents on sofas in the living room. After a lot of fussing and ushering the show would begin: a random selection of singing and dancing with a bit of miming and a lot of serious faces. I particularly enjoyed being the booming voice from behind the door: 'And noooooooow, ladies and gentlemen, for our *first act*...!' It was full-on *X Factor* style!

I must admit the shows were generally not great: I don't think any of us would have troubled *Britain's Got Talent*. But they were fun, despite the way we all took it so seriously, and the younger kids on the street would be beside themselves with excitement when they were allowed to join in. The final performance itself never really matched up to the hours we spent planning and rehearsing: that was where the real fun was. My finest hour was probably the time I decided to treat the family to my interpretation of Michael Jackson's 'Earth Song'. I get the giggles thinking of it now – me holding myself between the doorframes at home, swishing and swooshing my hair around for full effect. 'What about the elephants?' I'd be singing, looking incredibly pained. As ever, the assembled audience took it all very well, cheering and whooping. I am fairly sure I only saw my mum trying to contain her giggles a couple of times.

Slowly that taste for performance overtook my desire to climb trees. Both were just a different version of my constant quest for a fresh challenge, but the performing took off as I hit my teens. I had always been to local singing and dancing groups and as I started at secondary school, Hillview School for Girls in Tonbridge, the school gained performing arts status, which meant they built a theatre there. I loved school, but I can't claim to have been very good at the sitting still and listening element to learning. My attention span is ridiculously short and I have to keep moving and having fresh ideas or I really struggle to maintain interest. My grades were always good though, with a nice selection of As and Bs, which kept my parents happy – just as long as I could keep up the singing and dancing too, otherwise I'd go nuts.

As GCSEs loomed into view we were told that a representative from the BRIT School was coming to look round our school, with an eye out for kids to audition for places there. Immediately, I was really keen. I wasn't sure what I wanted to do after the exams – I was predicted the grades to go on and study for A-levels, but I wasn't sure whether I really wanted to study more in such a traditional way. But I wasn't any more convinced by the idea of getting a full-time job at that age either, so I figured that I would have nothing to lose if I gave the BRIT School a go. I did a drama piece which the representative saw. I threw myself into it; excited by the idea that I was being given an opportunity to do something I really loved. They must have picked up on my enthusiasm and of course they must have heard about my constant appearances in local shows. Not long afterwards, I was approached and invited to do a formal audition.

At the time of the audition, I hadn't really been out of my local area much. The idea that somewhere as prestigious as the BRIT School might take me seriously seemed almost fantastical. Not because I might not have the talent, but because I hadn't even realised there could be such opportunities out there. My world had rarely extended much further than my street or at most my town, so the idea of doing full-time drama and dance seemed out of my league. The more nervous I became, the more I tried to reassure myself that it would probably come to nothing. Repeating this to myself helped me to feel more fearless about the audition process: not just the nerves involved in the audition itself, but in admitting to my friends and family that this was what I wanted. For the first time in my life, I was sticking my neck out for real, taking the chance that I might become a smaller fish but in a much bigger pond. Deep inside, I hoped that I could reach that place and I believed that I stood a chance.

At the audition I was asked to perform three different types of dance – jazz, classical and contemporary. On top of that, I   had to perform one dance I'd choreographed myself and one that the school just threw at me, there and then. That day I felt as if I really was living *Flashdance*: *The Reality*. OK, my hair wasn't quite so big, but the moves were there. Looking back on it, I suppose that part of the challenge was similar to the kind of thing I ended up doing at the Miss England competition, but at the time I just thought it was an unmissable experience, if only to see how far I got. I was ambitious, but at that stage my curiosity at being able to even get a glimpse of this world, let alone take part in it, was overwhelming. I caught the train up to Selhurst with my mum and attended the audition, but then I was back at school the next day and pretty much forgot all about it. Or at least I tried to.

The week of my fifteenth birthday crept up on me, and one morning as I sat down to breakfast, I saw a letter by the front door. The postmark made it clear where it had come from: The BRIT School. I stared at it, looked around to see if anyone else had spotted it and glanced back at it again. No one else seemed to have noticed it. My hands were shaking as I went to pick up the envelope: I was either going to receive a real lifeline for my future, or I would have all the hopes that I had tried so hard to keep to myself dashed. I held the envelope up to the light just in case I could see inside and read the answer, but I couldn't. So I shoved it in my bag and got to school as quickly as I could. I wanted to find Hayley and open the envelope with her. Once I'd spotted her, I yanked her aside and we headed to the toilets to get some quiet. For once in my life I was quiet instead of chattering and squealing; I was temporarily silenced by the importance of the news I was about to receive.

And so I opened the envelope and read the letter: I had been offered a full scholarship! I could feel the excitement bubbling up from inside of me as I hugged Hayley and screamed, 'I did it!' I had been offered the chance of a future that I was genuinely excited by. But there was one final hurdle, which meant that I still wasn't sure if I would be able to go: the school was in Selhurst, Croydon and I lived in Kent. The travel would be expensive and the journey took a couple of hours, plus I was only just fifteen and wouldn't be much older by the time the term began.

I wanted to find a way to ensure that my parents would let me go; I wasn't about to be stopped at this stage in the plan. I worked out that there were some other kids in the local area who were older than me and would be attending the school, so I persuaded my parents to let me go with them. I would start in September 2002, the summer after I finished my GCSEs. To my joy, they said yes. That, however, didn't mean the journey was any shorter. For the entire time that I was at the BRIT School, I had to get up at five o'clock each day to catch a train leaving at 5.40am in order to arrive at school on time. It was pretty hardcore – I had never done such long days in my life. But the way I saw it, there was no alternative: I wanted to go to that school, so I was going to have to get there every day, rain or shine. There was also the fact that my parents were paying for my travel expenses – it was a struggle, but they coped because they knew it was something I was desperate to do.

Once I was there, I loved every minute of it. People often think that the BRIT School is just a load of wannabe pop stars prancing around in legwarmers checking their make-up, but we really studied hard. The day was dominated by dancing, singing and drama, and whenever we weren't in the studio we were studying the theory behind the practice. Our timetable was chopped up so we were never in the classroom for long enough for my attention to start wandering, and studying subjects like the theory of dance was a revelation to me. On the train home every evening I used to do my homework: I would arrive home exhausted and then get up to do it all again the next day, but I was in my element.

I was having so much fun every single day – I wouldn't have changed it for anything. A huge part of the experience was that my world suddenly seemed to get larger: after only ever hanging out with the kids in my area, I was now being exposed to proper London kids on a daily basis. Even moments like queuing for lunch in the canteen were exciting: there was a piano in there and while we were in line with our meal trays, someone would always sit down and start playing a song we'd been rehearsing. Before long, loads of us would start joining in and showing off to each other. It wasn't like any school I had ever dared to imagine before; it really was like the school in *Fame*.

The girls all seemed so much older than me and they had a real sense of style. Everyone at the BRIT School was very image-conscious and put thought into their 'look' every single day: if I was to fit in, my tomboy days would have to be a thing of the past. I started to consider how to dress to play up my own strengths and to think about what my best features were; I also wanted some new outfits. There was only one solution: I was going to have to get a part-time job.

And so I began my illustrious series of Saturday jobs by working in a bakery. Same as during the week, I had a 5am start on Saturdays and Sundays, only at the weekends I was done by 11am. Sadly, I only lasted in that job for about four months – not only because it was a bit boring and I kept burning my arms – but because I wasn't making any money. I just used to eat sausage rolls and doughnuts all day, then wonder where my wages had gone. It was pointless: baking a doughnut, eating a doughnut, baking a doughnut, eating a doughnut! I came home with barely a penny, thankful only that I managed not to put on any weight, probably because of all the running around I was doing. I loved those doughnuts and I still love them, but I learned my lesson about earning actual money and getting back some of what you put in.

My next job was at a call centre, where my friend Karen and I worked together. We were supposed to be those irritating people who ring up trying to offer you double-glazing, but we struggled with that, to say the very least. Both of us hated making the pestering calls, always feeling as if we were interrupting people. So instead, we'd sit around a desk with a list of people we were supposed to call, then put music on and chat to our so-called customers about whatever we wanted – which was usually anything but double-glazing. That job lasted longer than the bakery, maybe six whole months. To be honest, I was surprised we even made it so long.

But the part-time job I did actually apply myself to and enjoy was at JD Sports, where I was the weekend supervisor for trainers. A proper title at last! I had to try and sell people trainers and I was working on commission. The fact that I was up front in a busy store felt like a bit of a performance in itself and as I was always up for a challenge, I enjoyed trying to persuade people to make purchases. I was always up and about chatting with the steady flow of customers, so I never lost interest. Finally, I had found something that suited me but in the pit of my stomach I knew that dancing in the week and running round a sports shop at the weekend was a life that couldn't last forever.

I had been at the BRIT School for about a year and a half when I felt a slow realisation dawning on me: I had got my BTEC National Diploma in Performing Arts and was going on to do an Advanced Diploma. However, much as I loved life at the school, I wasn't convinced that I would be able to make a career out of performing. I could dance, I could act and I could just about sing, but I didn't excel at any of them. Unlike some of my fellow pupils, I wasn't standing out. While I was there, both Amy Winehouse and Katie Melua were students and left with megastar careers ahead of them. Those stars-to-be had always stood out from the crowd and it was obvious to me that I wasn't one of them.

More and more, I was coming to the realisation that the competition to survive, let alone succeed, in the world of performing arts was breathtakingly intense. Realistically, I would never be the next Britney Spears: becoming a Butlins Redcoat was as good as I was going to get and although I knew that would be fun for a bit, I was pretty sure that I would become bored after a while without a new challenge. I was going to have to work so hard just to make a living – let alone become a star – that I slowly began to wonder if it was, after all, the life for me. Although I had accepted my place as a way of enjoying school for a few more years and I had loved my time there, the fact that I was going to have to find a job more taxing than selling trainers was becoming unavoidable.

For now, I kept my concerns to myself while I was at home as I was still enjoying the day-to-day antics at the school and I didn't want to worry anyone. One weekend I was at home, enjoying a rare moment of lounging around in front of the TV with my family. My brother Byran was there, on leave from the Army, which he had joined in 2004. A break came in the programme we were all watching and an Army advert came on.

'Yeah, I reckon your job looks pretty easy,' I said, just to wind him up.

'Well, there's no way you'd be able to do it,' he replied. As far as he was concerned, I was just a silly little seventeen-year-old girl, a wannabe pop star with no idea what she was talking about. He was the serious-minded one, while I was the kid. But the way he dismissed me, quickly followed by the family all joining in with the teasing, struck a chord: had I boxed myself into being

15

nothing but a one-dimensional teen star? Was staying at the BRIT School limiting me to only one career, and one that I might not excel at? Suddenly I felt as if walls were closing in on me a little: I wanted to be more than just a silly girl that people could brush off so readily – and I knew that I could be.

Not long after that weekend I was chatting to my friend Leonie about our futures and I casually mentioned that joining the Army looked really easy, and more to the point, that it looked quite good fun too. I'd be out and about a lot, moving around the world, being presented with fresh challenges. The more I thought about it, the more it seemed like something I might actually love to do. In mentioning it to a girl friend, I suppose I was testing out the idea to myself: was I crazy to be considering it? Perhaps I was only thinking about it to annoy my brother. Was it just a knee-jerk reaction to the theatrical antics of life at the BRIT School? It felt as if I was feeling my way into a whole new mindset.

Again, the reply was a dismissive, 'Yeah right, Kat.' Except this time Leonie added: 'You simply would not be able to cope with the discipline, the food, anything. You would not be able to hack it. One. Little. Bit.'

And so it seemed that the consensus was that I shouldn't even give it a second thought. What more did I need to do to prove them all wrong? It was as if I was seven all over again, standing at the bottom of an enormous tree as those around me teased me, suggesting that there was no way I'd be able to climb it. The old emotions came flooding back, stronger than ever. 'So, you don't think I can do it? Then I'll give it all I've got,' I vowed to myself. The next day I went into town and made my first visit to the Army Careers Office: it turned out that it wouldn't be my last.

CHAPTER TWO

THE ARMY

FOLLOWING the jibes from my brother and my mate Leonie, I got myself down to the Army Careers Office faster than you could say 'GI Jane'.

I knew exactly where it was: next to the swimming pool in town that I'd been to hundreds of times as a child. I could remember walking past it, hand in hand with my classmates, as our little crocodile shuffled down to swimming class. For years, I thought there was a whole Army barracks in there, like those secret rooms in the James Bond movies, where an innocent-looking door is opened and – ta-da! – reveals an enormous training room full of men in black suits, doing martial arts and rifle practice. It was only years later when I decided to take the Army seriously that I realised it wasn't quite like that.

I didn't know what to expect from a first interview, so I

made sure I dressed smartly in a pencil skirt, a proper blouse and heels. I looked like a businesswoman, not a potential soldier, but it was my way of trying to show how seriously I was taking things. How wrong I was. The impression was more Miss Moneypenny than James Bond by the time I tottered off down the road.

As I left the house, I made sure I let my mum know where I was going. 'OK, darling, have a nice time,' she told me in an overly polite tone, but I knew she was just humouring me. 'We'll hear about this at the end of the day.' I could almost hear her thinking, 'Ah well, another one of Kat's crazy plans,' as I closed the door behind me.

As you approach the Army Centre, there's a large tank at the crossroads and a huge gate. Before you can go anywhere you have to press a buzzer to be let into the guardroom. I pressed it and heard an electronic voice.

'Hello?'

'Oh, um, hi. I'm here about an... er... Army career.' My own voice was squeaky with nerves: where had the confident girl, determined to prove everyone wrong, gone?

The massive metal gate swung open and I clip-clopped my way through to the guardroom to sign in. I can still remember the guard's face as he sat there in his Army uniform, looking me up and down. He must have been about forty years old, well built, with a stern look: he had the kind of features that looked as if they'd seen it all. I felt his gaze as he worked his way up from my heels to my blonde hair and he almost looked as if he was trying to stop himself from shaking his head. He might as well have had 'Yeah, whatever. What do you think you are doing here?' tattooed on his forehead. But I heard the gate slamming behind me and realised there was no turning back: I couldn't bail out now.

It was bad enough that my brother, my best mate and even my mum didn't think anything would come of this visit but now a complete stranger was staring at me, making it perfectly obvious that he thought my plan was pointless too. However, I felt that little buzz of determination inside: I was going to show him, I'd show them all! I explained that I'd like to speak to someone about joining the Army.

'Well, you'd better follow me then,' he told me, as he got out from behind the desk, his solid body looking even more intimidating without the furniture between us. The two of us set off down a maze of corridors; I had no idea where we were going and in my heels, was almost having to trot to keep up with his purposeful stride. I suspected he was trying to outpace me as I heard the soft squeak, squeak, squeak of his rubber combat boots on the lino flooring. Behind him, the tap-tap, tap-tap, tap-tap from my heels was going twice as fast. There was no conversation to hide the giveaway noises.

Too late, I thought to myself. I've just got to keep on walking.

At one point we passed a big gym filled with people circuit training. As I saw it, I felt a little bit more at home.

I felt encouraged to have seen people doing physical activity rather than sitting in a room full of desks, like most jobs; that was part of the reason why I was hoping to join up. I made sure I didn't seem unprofessional, though and kept up with the soldier as his rubber boots strode on.

Eventually we reached a door with a few chairs outside of it and my new friend nodded his head towards them, indicating that I should sit down. Then he left me. As I sat down, I noticed a side table covered in leaflets, just like when you're at the dentist or doctor. Out of curiosity, I picked up a couple of them and realised for the first time that there seemed to be all sorts of different things that you could do in the Army. Until that moment, I had thought that if you were in the Army – well, you were just in the Army. You rolled around in the mud, wearing green and holding a gun. What more was there?

As I sat there flicking through the leaflets, it felt as if I was being made to wait forever. Finally a woman came to the door. My heart sank. I don't think it would be unfair to describe her as vaguely butch – she strongly reminded me of Miss Trunchbull from Roald Dahl's *Matilda*. She was beyond a stereotype, and I began to wonder if I really did have a career in the British Forces. I could almost hear her thinking, what have we got here? Admittedly my Miss Moneypenny outfit may not have helped her warm to me, but I refused to feel intimidated, no matter how low I might be feeling.

'Right then, take a seat,' she said. And so I sat facing her large desk. Her chair was large and higher than mine. I felt like a schoolgirl, sitting on the low plastic chair. On the desk was a pace stick on a stand with a plaque with her name mounted on it. At the time I had no idea what it was – it just looked like two walking sticks, or a massive set of compasses. I could still tell it was pretty scary, but I didn't know then that it was a ceremonial item to symbolise authority. Originally it was used to measure the length of soldiers' paces as they march on parade.

The walls were a totally bland eggshell colour, but covered in plaques, awards, recruiting posters and photographs of 'Miss Trunchbull' in uniform. Out of the corner of my eye I could see what seemed to be a box room or a broom cupboard. What on earth was that random room for? I wondered to myself. As I looked behind her, I could see out of the window to the road and fields I knew from my childhood. There's my escape, I let myself think – but only for a moment!

'So have you any idea what you'd like to be in the Army?'

'Yes, I'd like to be, well, just, in the Army,' I replied. 'You know, where you dress in green and stuff?'

'Rii-iight!'

Then there was a pause while she looked down at my CV and saw that I had a small amount of experience in military pursuits in the Sea Cadets.

'Have you not thought about the Navy or the RAF then?' she asked, responding to this.

Her scowl, plus the thought of her judging me made me

want to play along and pretend to be even more girly than I really am. OK, I admit that I wanted to wind her up, and the heat of her disapproval added to my sense of wanting to make an impression.

'Oh no,' I replied. 'I really want to go for the Army as green is so much more my colour.'

There was a pause, filled only with silence. 'Miss Trunchbull' frowned, convinced she had nothing more than a flake on her hands. She wasn't softening: she was expecting me to fail. I felt as if she was thinking, 'You madam, are everything we don't need in the Army. It's sweet that you've popped over to see us, but good luck with the rest of your life'.

But she didn't say that: she just gave a quiet 'Mmm-hmm' and presented me with some forms to fill out. Because I was under eighteen, I had to take a form for my parents to fill in to prove that they were happy for me to join the Army and I was not just running away from home.

Then she looked at me calmly, straight in the eye and said: 'Now go away and think about this. Have a proper think, make sure that this really is what you want to do.' She gave me an appointment to come back the next week and said that if I didn't turn up, then she'd understand that I'd decided that Forces life just wasn't for me.

She couldn't have given me a better get-out clause.

And so I left the room and tottered off, just glad to be out of the situation. I breathed a sigh of relief to be away from the judging gaze of 'Miss Trunchbull', but instead of leaving the premises deflated, I was more determined than ever to prove her wrong. The minute I was on the other side of those metal gates I was on the phone to my friends, telling them: 'I've joined the Army.'

They didn't need to know that I hadn't actually done anything beyond going to an interview. I figured that the more people I told, the harder it would be for me to back out of the plan. Then I went into town and saw my boss in the sports shop, cheerily announcing that I'd be leaving work soon as I was joining the Armed Forces.

'Yes, Kat,' she replied. 'We'll see you next Saturday, shall we? Until you've got confirmation, let's not get too formal with the notice, hmm?'

But I went home, took the forms to my mum and asked her to sign them.

'If this is what you really want to do,' she said. I nodded and urged her that I did. And so the next week I was back in 'Miss Trunchbull's' office. Though unwavering in my desire to impress her, I wasn't about to compromise – I went in an outfit that was just as smart as the time before. Another pencil skirt and blouse. The way I saw it, this was a job interview and I couldn't turn up wearing the kind of clothes that you'd normally attend training camp in.

To my relief, she seemed a lot more approachable this time. Perhaps she was taken aback that I had actually turned up. I suppose she was used to seeing a lot of timewasters, or people who weren't suitable for the Army and just fancied looking around the building on a whim.

First of all, we had a proper discussion about life in the Armed Forces and she was taking me much more seriously. She asked lots of questions about my life, how my parents got on, whether I had ever done drugs, if I had a criminal record, what my hobbies were, what sports I was into. I felt a bit odd explaining to her that I was at stage school but she didn't seem too bothered by that, just pleased that I was doing something with myself.

And she was quite impressed that I had been to Sea Cadets. I also had to take in my GCSE certificates and she was pleased to see what good grades I had. Then I mentioned that my brother had joined the Army a couple of years before, and she realised that she had recruited him too. Slowly, she was looking down her nose at me a bit less.

'It's great that you've come back,' she told me with a smile. 'Have you had a chance to take a look at the booklets?'

I admitted that I had had a good look, but that I was still not really sure what I wanted to do. In truth, at this point I was chasing acceptance not experience. Consequently it didn't really matter to me what role I would be performing so I had just looked up which ones seemed the easiest to pass.

'Don't worry about that – when you come to do the BARB test, it will enable us to see which jobs might be suited to you,' I was told.

The British Army Recruit Battery test – or BARB test for short – checks your ability to understand information and solve problems in your head. This helps the Army match you with roles that most suit your abilities. It's a touch-screen test and you can't really fail it, but I was still quite nervous about taking it.

It's a little bit like the driving theory test or those Nintendo DS memory games and it is designed to see how quickly you react to situations, remember things or solve problems. The test is split into five sections: Reasoning, Letter Checking, Number Distance, Odd One Out and Symbol Rotation. You are asked a series of questions, such as 'Paul is stronger than Pete', followed by 'Who is weaker?' and the idea is to click on names as fast as you can. There are shapes to sort and numbers to add, too.

I was shown into a booth to the side of the room, which had an enormous computer in it. It looked like the old Amstrad 64, the ones with the tape that you had to turn over halfway through the game. After sitting down, I put on the enormous headphones, my nervousness just about stopping me from smirking at the retro computer.

I took a practice test first, and then completed the real thing. Slowly, the giant computer printed out the results from a machine just as sophisticated. The slow dzzz-dzzz-dzzzz as the pages scrolled out was agony, as I sat in the room with only 'Miss Trunchbull' for polite conversation. Taking the test had left me all fired up, though. And as it turned out, I'd got a great score of around 65 – the average is 50 – and my confidence was given a huge boost.

The end result was that I could do any job suitable for a female in the Army. Of course I was thrilled, but that didn't really help me: I still couldn't decide what I wanted to do.

One of the key roles that women are currently excluded from in the Armed Forces is the Infantry. The Infantry are the main ground soldiers on the frontline who generally move on foot and fight the enemy using rifles at close quarters. At first I was disappointed that I couldn't be in the Infantry as that was what I'd seen my brother do and I wanted to be included as much as possible. But 'Miss Trunchbull' explained to me everyone in the Army is a soldier first and the decision that I was currently making was to do with what trade I wanted to learn. She gave me the list and instructed me to go away and have a proper think. Meanwhile, she was going to set me up with my two-day selection weekend date.

That was also the day when she handed me the Fitness Book. It stated that it might be two months before was called up for a selection weekend, but it could be as soon as two weeks' time. Clearly, I needed to immediately get started on a proper fitness regime and the bit that worried me most was the running: it really wasn't my strong suit.

It would have been awful to have my fitness let me down once I'd done so well in the BARB test. Long-distance running I was always good at, and I knew I was quite fit from all the dancing at the BRIT School, but because the Fitness Book said I had to do a mile and a half in less than 14 minutes, I started to panic. And I was right to do so: my initial times were rubbish and there was no way I would have passed without training.

The booklet also mentioned press-ups. I had tried to do one press-up in my life and failed miserably; it was shocking. The night before I had gone for that first interview my mind was swimming with movie images of soldiers face down in the mud, working out. I thought: 'Hmm, I've never actually tried a press-up. Let's have a go'. So I lay down on my bedroom floor and had a go at doing one, but it was a disaster. 'Ngggggggggggg!' My arms started to shake and judder under the strain. Soon I collapsed on the floor, grazing my chin and staring at the carpet. I had a problem on my hands. Literally. The booklet was telling me that I needed to do a minimum of 21 full press-ups, not on my knees or anything, within two minutes.

Sit-ups – fine, I had a strong core from all the dance training, but the other one that made me laugh was pull-ups. You'd think I might have nice strong arms after all those years of hoisting myself up trees but you'd be wrong. 'Going to have to work on those two,' I thought to myself. So, how do you practise at home? Well, you can't: I managed three.

But I didn't have any experience as a runner and I didn't want to be seen as having only 'girly' skills: I wanted to score a good time for my run and so I hatched a plan. I prepared for it by persuading my dad to regularly get me in the car, tap on the odometer and drive me a couple of miles from home, then dump me outside and leave me to run back, remembering the route. It was a fun, bonding thing between us. Depending on the time of night and the traffic, we would sometimes have a race and occasionally I'd manage to beat him back, which was exceedingly satisfying. I'd keep timing myself. I also worked out that my dad's office was exactly a mile and a half from home so I would sometimes run there and get a lift from him.

At first, I was aiming for a time of 11.5 minutes and when I began, I couldn't make it in less than 14, so I really did need to do some training. By the time I got to selection day, I was just about getting to 11.30 although it was a scrape every time. I was really panicking that I wouldn't make it on the day, but decided to put a bit of faith in adrenaline.

Meanwhile, I was also obsessed at being able to do as many press-ups as were thrown at me. After all, doesn't every movie ever to feature a woman in training have a scene where she collapses, unable to cope with the press-ups? I didn't want that woman to be me: I wanted to prove that I deserved a place – I wasn't going to let myself become a cliché.

About a week into my training I was given the date for my selection weekend. It was to be held in late May 2004 and so I had about eight weeks to prepare. I was sent an information pack with the date, what to pack and a train ticket, so that I was all set: I had to take three sets of sports kit, a suit for the interview and smart/casual clothes for the evening function on the night that we stayed. Meanwhile, I was so determined about my training that my family had started to take me slightly more seriously. Only slightly, mind: the night before I set off, my mum sat me down for a chat.

'Now don't be too disappointed if you don't get selected, will you?'

'Well, I'm really trying not to think like that…'

'I'm just saying, it might not be for you and we all want you to know that no one will be disappointed in you. We just want you to be happy.'

The trouble was, by this stage nothing short of gaining a place in the Armed Forces would make me happy. I had worked too hard already.

Things were moving fast, and more and more, I was starting to imagine myself in the Army. It wasn't just the adventure that was now filling my mind, but the value of being a soldier. The more I learned about the job, the more I realised that heroism was evident in spades, all around me and every day – and from people who might always remain unheard of, despite their amazing efforts. There's never going to be a world pop-star shortage, but the importance and need for good soldiers was becoming clearer to me and so my determination was taking on a different edge.

The day finally came and I got the train from Tonbridge into London. I then had to catch a second one down to Pirbright in Surrey. My information pack had told me that someone would meet me at the station. As I sat on the train to Pirbright, I looked around, examining everyone else on the carriage to try and work out if they were going on the course too. I was checking out their luggage, how nervous they looked, if they looked like competition or not, but I didn't spot anyone who looked a likely candidate to me. Then again, what does someone who might soon be in the Army look like? I'm sure no one would have chosen me from a line-up that day.

When the train pulled in and I collected my bag from the rack, a sudden thought hit me: who is collecting me? How will I recognise them? Panic rushed through my veins as I left the train but I soon realised that I needn't have worried for there was a man in Army uniform standing by a mini-bus. Standing around him were about thirty people, looking just as nervous as I felt. One panic had been replaced by another.

As we boarded the bus, I spotted another girl. We sat down next to each other and I smiled at her.

'What's your name, then?'

'Amy. Yours?'

'Kat. And phew, I'm not the only girl!'

Amy had curly hair that had been done nicely, she had make-up on and she looked like someone I could work alongside and be friends with, rather than a person that I might be intimidated by. There were other girls there with short hair and very serious expressions, but I was so thrilled that Amy and I had found each other and we weren't totally outnumbered.

The drive to the camp felt like the longest journey ever. We were all chatting, but I sensed that everyone just wanted to arrive and get on with things. When we reached the camp, it was my first real experience of entering a genuine working barracks. The guards were at the gate, there were soldiers marching across camp in formation. It was like being driven onto the set of a Hollywood movie: all the props you could imagine were there.

We were shown to our rooms and they certainly weren't pretty. They were proper military dormitories: rooms for eight, filled with four bunk beds on which were placed the thinnest mattresses imaginable, with the scratchiest blankets I've ever known folded at the end of them.

'So those are your rooms. Now get changed into sports kit!' was all that we were told. We were then thrown coloured bibs with numbers on them – I hadn't seen anything like it since I'd played netball as a kid. We were to be tested throughout the day, so we weren't allowed to take our bibs off at any point. I had a brand new sports kit on underneath the dreaded bib, though which made me feel less of an anonymous number. I was still Kat under there! And of course, I still did my best with my hair and make-up, although I had pinned my hair up.

First up was the medical, when it dawned on me for the first time how hard these tests were actually going to be. I was near the end of the queue but was quickly informed that they were doing all sorts of tests, such as measuring our body fat, hearing tests, sight tests and checking for asthma, heart conditions and all sorts. At the start of the selection process, there were about eighty of us, but by the time we left the medical centre, thirty had already gone. The experience felt like the X *Factor* knockout stages: it literally was boot camp.

Almost immediately, the group had been almost halved: it was impossible not to notice both men and women occasionally coming out of the room crying and this was only making the waiting candidates even more nervous. Some had come all the way across the country only to be told to turn around and head back again after a ten-minute medical. I really felt for them but most of all, I hoped it wouldn't happen to me; I found myself wanting to be accepted because of the Army itself, not just because I wanted to prove my doubters wrong. What started out as almost a joke had kick-started a new career.

While we were waiting nervously, I spent as much time as I could with Amy. Thank God I found her! We were torn between wanting to chat and giggle, and swapping notes about how we were getting along, what we thought of the others and what was next, while trying to look as serious and professional as we could at all times. Even though we were allowed to talk, everyone was keeping it to a minimum.

After the medical those of us left were taken to a conference-type room for an ice-breaker exercise: we had to take it in turns to head to the front and talk about ourselves for two minutes. Then we'd be asked questions by the rest of the group. Basically, it was a confidence exercise. Some of the people in the group were, to be honest, no real competition for Alan Carr in the chattiness department, but the thing that really surprised me was how many seemed truly terrified by it. Men who had been looking confident all day – classic Army types with rippling muscles and neat short hair – just stared at their feet and stammered. But this exercise was also to make sure that we were as interested as possible in everyone else. We were being tested both ways – talking and listening, so we couldn't just sit there sneering.

Once the icebreaker was over we were given horrible blue overalls, a helmet and some random planks of wood. We were then divided into groups of eight and ushered outside to a wooded area. I had no idea what was coming next and I was starting to wonder why I'd brought brand new trainers. We were told it was called a 'command task' but what this resembled most was *Big Brother*'s weekly tasks: 'Get from A to B without touching the grass' and other things like that.

I felt lucky as I was with quite a lot of shy people – I couldn't believe no one else was speaking up more; we were there to be tested. It suited me though as I was able to take control and suggest things: 'Come on, Number 7, move the rope over here!' I was standing there balanced on a log, trying to throw a length of rope and I was damned if someone else's shyness was going to get in my way. After all, I still had the run to do tomorrow and I wasn't going to fall and injure myself on anyone's account. People, get a grip!

Meanwhile, Army examiners with notepads were standing around, judging us. I could see them making sly eye contact with each other about who was doing well and who wasn't, like Sir Alan Sugar's henchmen in *The Apprentice*. It made me keener than ever to show that I really meant it when I said I was Army material.

By the end of the day I was exhausted, but we went off to shower and change out of our sports clothes. Then it was off to an Army-style cookhouse for the first time. We didn't just turn up, though: we had to *march* there! It was the first time that I had ever attempted anything like that and we stuck out like sore thumbs in our civilian clothes. I was wearing my 'safety blanket outfit' that I like to wear when I'm dressing formally for an event – another pencil skirt and blouse – and I could feel the gaze of the existing soldiers on camp as they saw us straggling along, attempting to march for the first time. It was like trying to ride your bike without stabilisers for the very first time in front of the other kids from the street.

I struck up conversations with some of the others as we were sitting down having our dinner and was surprised by all the different answers and reasons why people wanted to be in the Army. Some, like my new friend Amy, had wanted to do it forever. Others couldn't think of a job that they wanted to do and had chosen the opportunities for travel and education that the Army provided. I was surprised by how many had military families and wanted to do what their parents or siblings did. What united us was the desire for a challenge rather than a normal desk job. I felt as if I was among people who knew how I felt: I had found my kind of people.

But even with the distraction of the tests, the friends I was making and the effort of learning to march (badly), at the back of my mind was a constant voice, telling me: 'Tomorrow you've got to do the run. Tomorrow you've got to do the run. Tomorrow you've got to do the run…'

When I pulled the itchy blanket over me in my bunk that evening, I was convinced I'd never sleep in a bed so uncomfortable. And I was so nervous about being rested for the physical challenge that I started to panic: I wanted my own comfy bed and my mum. But the day had exhausted me and I fell asleep the minute my head touched the lumpy pillow.

The next thing I knew, a stranger had walked into the room and turned the harsh strip lights on. 'Time for your run!' was all we were told. It was 5am – time to get up if you're an Army recruit.

I felt physically sick, I was so nervous. We went to breakfast but I just pushed it around my plate. It was greasy eggs and bacon – the last thing I wanted was to see it again if I was going to vomit on the running track.

Before we reached the track we were taken to the gym for sit-ups and press-ups. The first batch was fine. Even though there was someone watching us like a hawk, I knew that I was strong enough to get through the sit-ups. Then came the press-ups: I managed about three. What I wish I'd known then was that they weren't really counting to see how many you could do, but to make sure that you tried your absolute hardest at every point. Anyone who panicked and gave up, or didn't seem to be giving it their all was on more dangerous ground than those who needed to get fitter, but were showing a bit of grit.

Then it couldn't be delayed any longer: the run. Unbelievably we had to do an 800m warm-up first. I had had no idea about that bit and was already huffing by the time that I completed it. It was a cold, grey morning and the kind of surprise that I could have done without.

As we stood at the starting line I found myself thinking: what am I doing? Why am I putting myself through this? I was genuinely unhappy – it was freezing, no one thought I could do it and I was sick with nerves. But there was no point in sulking off: I had to get a hold of myself. If I asked to go home at this point, the shame would be too enormous. It was time to show them – and myself – what I was truly made of.

'Ready, steady, GO!'

My training had taught me that I needed to keep a constant pace rather than sprint off and immediately exhaust myself. But I was also aware that I'd never done this route before and I wouldn't know when I was halfway: the route went round the camp twice, finishing with one long drag. It felt like the longest track ever. Some people were clearly faster than me and streaked ahead. What did they have for breakfast?! There was no way I could ever run that fast. But others started to straggle behind. Bewildered by the new location as opposed to the familiar roads around my house, I lost all perspective of whether I was going at my usual pace. Eventually, I made it to the end but my feet felt like blocks of pure lead. I was pumping my arms back and forth to try and propel myself forward as fast as possible while my lungs felt as if they were on fire. By the time that I crossed the finishing line, I was ready to collapse in a delirious mixture of relief, panic and exhaustion. I had no idea how well I'd done – they didn't tell us our times. All I could do was to catch my breath and hope for the best.

The final part of the test was our interviews: one by one, a senior officer called us in for the interview and I was painfully aware that this person was about to decide the fate of my career. It was the X *Factor* Simon Cowell moment and worst of all, they would tell us if we had been selected at the end of the interview. This time, there would be no sneaking off to the bathroom to read the letter, unlike my BRIT School application: I was going to be told, face-to-face.

While in the shower getting ready to change into my suit I felt consumed by tiredness. I was ready to go home: I had given the physical challenges my all and I wasn't sure that I would even be able to make sense in the interview. As I sat outside waiting, the tension mounted. Some, who I had been sure would get in, were coming out in tears. Amy came out with a huge grin, having been granted an unconditional place. Others were told that they were in, but that they were more suited to a different type of job within the Army.

As I sat down, the first thing I was asked was: 'So how do you think you did?'

'I don't know!' was all I could blurt out at first. And then: 'Well, I don't know how my times were, but I know that I did the absolute best I could' – trying to sound cautious and confident at the same time. At the very least I know I could look them in the eye, knowing there was nothing more that I could have done to try harder.

Rather than just telling me how I'd done, the men in the panel in front of me just nodded enigmatically.

'Let's look at the stages, shall we? The icebreaker. How do you think you did there?'

'I don't care any more! Just tell me!' was all I wanted to yell. But I smiled and went through each stage patiently, stressing that my stage school training had given me confidence and communication skills rather than making me a girly flake.

'Right, so you want to join the Adjutant General's Corps?' (A scribble on a notepad). 'And you seemed to enjoy the Command Task.' (A quick glance at some notes). 'And your run time was...'

But I didn't catch what the time was. And even if I had, my ears were ringing with nervousness. I was pressing my nails into the inside of my palms, hoping that my smile still seemed bright and positive. Meanwhile, I could hear the hushed hustle and bustle on the other side of the door. Was I going to be one of the ones who shuffled out trying to avoid eye contact, scuttling away and reluctant to discuss the reason why I had been denied a place? Or was I going to find Amy with a grin?

'Well, we're pleased to say that we would very much like to offer you a place in the British Armed Forces.'

'Thank you!' And I had to stop myself from leaping across the desk and hugging them all. I had proved everyone wrong: my family, my friends and my colleague. Hard work had won me a place and I didn't hesitate to accept my position.

There was one small problem: at this point I hadn't really absorbed the fact that acceptance meant that I would actually be in the Army. When I was told that I'd be contacted soon with a date to start my basic training, for a moment I almost felt confused. Was I going to be up to the challenge full-time?

But any doubts vanished as I grabbed my mobile from my bag on the way home. I called everyone I could think of to tell them my news and the more I said it, the more I realised that I had had an enormous buzz from the daily challenge on the selection weekend. But I could already hear the jibes from my brother: 'Well, it's not *that* hard to get a place. Can you get through the training, though?' By the time I got home, all I could think was: *Bring it on*!

The next morning I headed to the sports shop and handed in my resignation. I wasn't surprised by the response: 'Well, if you get there and you can't handle the training, you know you will always have a place here.' A backhanded compliment if ever there was one. Even on my last day there, everyone joked to me: 'See you in a couple of weeks!' What would it take to shut everyone up?

I was due at the training camp on 24 June and my mum and Irene, a family friend, took me for lunch at a nearby pub the day before. We called it 'The Last Supper' as Winchester was going to be my home for the next 12 weeks. No one knew exactly where I'd be after that. The reality that I might be sent to a war zone within a few months had not yet hit home: since being accepted, I had been excited about the challenge of training for the next six weeks and had thought no further than that. Even news reports about the Iraq war, which had recently begun, did not seem like something that could actually happen to me.

As usual, I paid intense attention to my shopping and packing: I was wearing a new suit, new kitten heels and had a new, hot-pink suitcase. Joining the Army is not an excuse to let standards slip. No way! My hair and make-up were also perfect. Why abandon attention to detail?

The arrival policy was that as you didn't have official identification documents yet, you had to report to the front desk and explain that you were there for basic training. As I waved goodbye to my mum and stepped towards the gate, my stomach was full of knots. Smiling to hide my nerves, I dragged the suitcase along behind me as I tottered forward on my heels. If there was one thing the BRIT School had taught me, it was that looking as good as I could, smiling and putting my best foot forward was the best way to keep nerves at bay and so I held my head up high and vowed to do my best.

But perhaps my best wasn't the Army's best. Across the drill square came a bellowing male voice: 'Oh my God, lads!' it echoed to everyone in the area. 'Combat Barbie's arrived!'

The remark was duly followed by raucous laughter from everyone who had heard him. Although I didn't know it at the time, at that moment a nickname for life had been created. I heard the laughter of the soldiers, but decided not to be offended by it: I knew I'd earned the right to be there. So as long as I wasn't being disrespectful, I could have whatever suitcase and hairstyle I wanted, as long as my hair was a natural colour and kept in a bun or off the collar. Why did I need to look a certain way to be in the Army now that I knew I had the skills they required?

And so I was led to the sleeping quarters. Once again, I was in a dormitory for eight, filled with girls. I looked around: this time, there were no girls like Amy. These were not girly girls. A moment of panic flitted across my mind – would this lot take me seriously? And then I spotted the girl who has been my best friend ever since: Stacey.

For a start, she had letterbox-red streaks in her hair. She was wearing a stylish suit and had perfect make-up. Our eyes met. 'What's your name?' we asked each other at exactly the same time. We had the same fear: being the only girly girl in the Army. Finding Stacey gave me the reassurance that I needed as I arrived on camp but, well, you could say it also made me a little too relaxed. To this day I still cringe when I think about what happened next.

We were instructed to get into our PE kit and I gleefully got out another of my new outfits, especially purchased for my new life. This time it was a bright pink tracksuit with matching accessories. I tied my hair (blonde at the time) back into two bunches, high up on the top of my head – I don't know what I was thinking; I looked more like someone hoping to be an extra in a celebrity fitness video than a professional preparing to defend the nation.

And so I wandered downstairs into a room where everyone who was going to be in our troop were was waiting. There were about thirty of us, mainly men. The corporal in charge looked at me and then looked at Stacey, who was in a similar get-up.

'*You, you* – upstairs!' We could tell he was furious but we were too scared to even reply. 'Get the war paint off and sort the hair out, Barbie!'

His tone was one of utter scorn. Stacey and I just looked at each other. What had we let ourselves in for? We scurried upstairs, too embarrassed to even giggle about the situation. I would never have admitted it at the time and it's so shaming to do so now, but that day all I was thinking was, there are so many guys down there – I don't want them to see me looking ugly. Do I have to take my make-up off?

All my friends had been teasing me about how I would have the best pulling opportunities in any job, ever. And I had only just realised how much I cared. Having said that, it didn't take long after getting back downstairs with a freshly scrubbed face before I realised that they were just guys, the same as anywhere else. They weren't any more special than the ones I met at school or out on the town with my mates and before long, they seemed more interested in their new job and whether I could do mine than anything else.

Something else I quickly noticed after looking around the room was that I was definitely one of the youngest there. Most were in their twenties but some looked in their late-twenties. It turned out that this was what I was more self-conscious about. From across the room, I spotted a lad who looked about my age.

'How old are you?' I mouthed at him.

He held up two flat palms and then seven fingers. Seventeen! The same age as me. We grinned at each other and later in the day, we got chatting. His name was Richard Hayes, but I've called him 'Haysey' from that day to this. We are still mates now, despite all the trouble we've got each other into over the years for chatting and messing around. At first, our seniors thought we were flirting with each other when we would sit and whisper during talks, but we were just relieved to have found someone our own age. We crack each other up too much to flirt, but that does mean we've had a fair few reprimands for not paying attention! To me, he is like a brother – someone I was always able to confide in when I was feeling low during training, and someone who has been a loyal friend ever since.

The next day we were marched down to be given our uniform. Humiliatingly, I had to wait two days later than everyone else as at the time I was super-skinny and none of the trousers fitted me. So, while everyone else was writing their name in indelible ink and being taught how to iron their brand new kit – the thick, hardwearing fabric still shiny – I remained in my pink tracksuit. No wonder the 'Combat Barbie' nickname stuck.

We were also taught how to lay our bed and locker area so that it was up to military standards. Our locker and bed was to form our entire personal living area for 12 weeks, so any mess or disorder was seen as a stain on our reputation and ability to keep up with the rest of the team. At first, I had all sorts of ideas about personalising the space, making sure it was a sanctuary from the chaos of training, but in hindsight I was missing the point: there was no escape, we were being taught to live as soldiers. I got as far as putting photos of my friends and family on the shelf behind the bed but the rest of the time I was too busy to do much other decorating. My stash of relaxing glamour-filled magazines went unread, my civvies unworn: it was 12 weeks of constantly living as soldiers, learning to think and act as them at all times. Even at the weekends we were in Army tracksuits, so we were constantly militarised. Being entirely absorbed into the system was what changed us from civilians to true soldiers.

And a true soldier I became – learning discipline, self-respect and how to form really tight friendships. The people I trained with knew what I had been through as they'd been there, too. Some of the best times were when we could bond over stupid stuff such as being allowed to play loud music while we did our ironing. Even a small treat like that seemed enormous in the context of the intense training that we were going through.

Every day was different; there was no set routine. One day we'd be learning to march, another it was how to shoot and take rifles apart, getting ready to go on exercise. Each morning we were on parade at 6am.

We'd be woken up by someone turning on the lights and then it was 10 minutes until we had to be out there: late at night we'd be mopping floors and folding clothes to make sure we could be up and out in time. As a result, when we were woken our uniform was in our locker positioned ready for us to just reach for it and get dressed, half asleep if need be. It was a 100 per cent change from the effort I had learnt to put into dressing at the BRIT School – and to the effort I'd find myself putting in when it came to the future. I have never forgotten the lesson so I can go from being sound asleep to fully dressed and performing my duty in under 10 minutes. Routine became crucial: blankets had to be at the perfect angle or they'd take your bed linen and throw it out of the window to teach you a lesson. Lockers must be locked or the same thing would happen.

What made the harshness of training bearable was that the consequences and implications of our actions were always explained to us. We had to be trained to get up and ready, quick as a flash with no man left behind, was because we might need to do so in a warzone. And we had to learn to support each other so that no one was left behind in a combat situation. It didn't always help, but knowing this was certainly inspiring.

Throughout the 12 weeks, people would peel away. One minute they were there, the next they had snapped, realised they couldn't cope and decided the humiliation of heading home without a qualification was preferable to continuing to train for a job they no longer believed they were suited to. This meant that the ones who stayed got even closer. If someone wasn't doing well and was dragging down the group, we couldn't just ignore them: we had to help them to keep up with us. If a person was awful then they'd be sent back to another group who had begun training later than us: the ultimate humiliation.

The lowest points were if you were doing well but someone else had messed up, because that still meant that we all got punished. We'd be out there in the pouring rain doing press ups, being screamed at as a group, for something that 90 per cent of us were in no way responsible for. Although it was helping us to build our relationship as a team, I used to feel such fury at carrying other people through the experience. Luckily I never let my anger show though, as on one occasion I really did mess up.

The first six weeks of training focused on us learning to march and for the second six weeks, we concentrated on doing so while carrying our rifle. When we were still learning to march, we would have to shout out rhymes and numbers to help keep us in beat and show the rest of the camp that we were still learning. (As if they couldn't tell, anyway!) It was grim having to march past recruits who were in their twelfth week, shouting, 'Left, Right! Left, Right!' as this was an instant way to draw attention to our inexperience. After a few weeks my group passed our first drill test, showing that we knew the basics of marching. Only a day after that we were marching to dinner when I saw what I thought was an officer. Obviously I was still a little hazy on what the various badges and stripes on our seniors' uniforms meant. But I was convinced that I had read it right and was a dazzlingly brilliant recruit for spotting him from afar. Erm, not so!

'Salute, guys, salute!' I quickly started whispering to the group. 'Come on, it's an officer, we've been taught how to salute, so now we have to!'

So we all did. Except we were not saluting an officer, as we quickly found out when he started shouting at us. Not only had I made a mistake, I'd persuaded everyone else to join in. It was one thing for me to bring shame on myself, but to drag the others down with me, and in such a bossy way, was a real betrayal of their trust. I had insisted that they do as I say, and I'd been utterly wrong. For the rest of the week I had the humiliation of being the only one to shout out the drill calls, wherever we went on camp. Each time I did it, my voice sounded sadder and more ashamed – I hated it. This ritual might not sound like much, but its purpose was to show me up in front of everyone on camp: my seniors, the recruits who had been training longer than us, and of course the recruits more junior than us. I had effectively been demoted – and publicly. It wasn't the ideal way of proving that 'Combat Barbie' could be more brains than blonde.

Without doubt, those were the hardest three months I have ever had. Now home comforts meant more than ever: there was one place where I could get phone signal and that was the very end of the rugby pitch. There was no chance of a sneaky text to my mum before bed – the best it got was that on a Saturday, if I had half an hour to myself then I would go to the end of the fields and call my friends and family for a bit. I missed them all so much that I would end up going out there, whatever the weather. Sometimes I was out on the pitch in howling gales and pouring rain, just desperate for a five-minute chat and a bit of encouragement from my mum, or some snippets of gossip from Hayley. It was the same place that we were sent to for exercises whenever we were in trouble as well, so it felt as if that patch of grass really had it in for me half the time.

Sometimes it seemed as if those in charge would make things up just to get us in trouble so that they could teach us about discipline: it really as a case of 'We've spotted some *dust* over there and it's *your* fault!' if ever they felt that one of us needed knocking down a peg or two. Some days we'd be out there on that rugby pitch in our best uniform, crawling around in the mud, just because one of the team had made a tiny mistake. Each time, we were all dragged out there just so that we'd learn the value of operating as a team. When I visited the barracks a couple of years later while working in a recruitment role, I shuddered to see the Rugby Pitch of Doom.

On most days of the training, I was tired to the point of tears but by the end of week twelve I was a transformed woman. On the final day, 31 October 2004, I was so proud to march off that drill square in front of my family and the crowd – I wanted to punch the air!

'*Yes*! All of you thought I could never do this!' was the one thought running through my mind as I marched past them. My family were so proud of me and they all congratulated me afterwards. And best of all, I knew that I finally had two weeks off.

Towards the end of our trade training we were told where our first postings would be. I was thrilled when I learnt that mine would be the same place as Stacey: the Royal Anglian Regiment, also based in Pirbright. Combat Barbie and Combat Sindy – as Stacey had by now been nicknamed – were ready to serve.

Within a month of accepting our posts, however, we were informed that one of us would be posted to Iraq. My heart sank at the thought of us being separated – we had been through everything together so far. Both of us were sent to do the requisite training and told that the decision on who would be going would be taken at a later date. I wasn't sure if I wanted it to be me or not, but news of this posting was the sudden wake-up call that we really were in the Army, and we were a country at war. Suddenly, being embarrassed on the drill square or not being able to make mobile phone calls seemed rather trivial when I might be heading for a warzone.

CHAPTER THREE

IRAQ TOUR

WE HADN'T joined the Army hoping to sit around in the British countryside, though: we had always known that there would be a chance that we'd be serving abroad, possibly in a warzone. So Stacey and I both threw ourselves into the specialist preparation that the whole regiment was doing for Basra. After all, neither of us knew which one of us would heading there nor would we want to let our pal down by slacking on the training – we had to support each other. Our fitness regimes were stepped up, we did extra rifle training and we went away on exercise a lot more. Also, we were repeatedly warned in training that as we were two girly girls, there would be a lot of lads out there who would be a bit bored and lonely, and might want to talk to us for one reason and one reason alone, so we must be on our guard. And the idea of going away with only men was even more nerve-wracking than the idea of the posting itself: the whole process further reinforced the fact that our job served a purpose and we had to be prepared to do it.

One day in March 2005, I was summoned to see my boss. After being told that it was me who would be going, I was excited, nervous and sad to be leaving Stacey behind because I knew she had worked so hard on the training too. Luckily, a couple of days later Stacey was informed that we'd both be going after all. '*Yessss!*' was our response. Sure, it came as a shock that I would be going so soon but to me, being in the Army and never serving in Iraq or Afghanistan would have been like being a hairdresser and never being allowed to cut hair: I wouldn't have felt as if I'd done my job properly. That was my opinion then, and it's my opinion now – it did little to ease my nerves, though.

It was April 2005 when we were due to leave, a time when there had been an increase in violence in Iraq. The Iraqi elections were also taking place, so there was a heightened sense of apprehension and anxiety in the area. Yes, our role was a peacekeeping one – we were largely there to help train the Iraqi Army to take over from us after the first democratic elections –   but this was only the very beginning of the process and we were still on rocky ground. It was a big year to go, and things were far from safe.

But I refused to allow fear to get in the way of the task

in front of me and so I tried to turn that switch off in my head. I knew that if I started to let nerves in, this might affect my performance and so I was determined not to fall victim to them.

As the TV news coverage continued daily, the entire country seemed anxious about the situation in Iraq and when my family learned that I would be going, they immediately started to worry about it too. I tried not to fuel their concerns by expressing my own, but what I was really scared of wasn't combat – something I had been trained for – but being kidnapped and beheaded. There had also been intelligence received that rebel Iraqis were specifically looking to kidnap female soldiers. Training had taught me to both support and rely on my fellow soldiers, so the idea of being taken from them terrified me.

Thankfully, I didn't have time to think about things too much as the regiment was leaving for Iraq in less than a month. I don't know what I would have done otherwise, but it worked in my favour that I didn't allow myself to fully absorb the fact that I was going to a warzone until I was actually in Iraq. Instead, like any sensible girl, I focused on packing.

When you are sent on tour to somewhere like Afghanistan or Iraq, you are allowed one large cardboard box of personal belongings between two people. These are then despatched to the camp ahead of you. Some people took laptops and PlayStations with them, but I was more interested in home comforts than distractions.

The first thing I packed was a pink duvet set so that even if I was sleeping in a tent, I could make my bed cosy. We were all taking military sleeping bags anyway, but if I was going to be in such a foreign, unfamiliar environment then I wanted to bring a little bit of homeliness with me.

Some of the other items that I packed really give the game away about how little I had absorbed about where I was actually going: my hair straighteners, a six-month supply of mascara, manicure kits, make-up remover, loads of hair accessories, and – worst of all – several bottles of fake tan! Really, I do not know what I was thinking: I was going to one of the hottest countries in the world – in uniform – and yet I still wanted to maintain a fake tan.

A couple of days before we flew out there, Stacey and I even went for a spray tan. The way we saw it, there would be so many soldiers on the camps who had been out there for months and we didn't want to look really white, like holidaymakers on their first day at the beach. That seems ridiculous now, but as ever, the way I coped with being nervous about a situation was to make sure that I made myself look as good – and appropriate – as possible. I just wanted to be sure my pale skin didn't make me stand out as an innocent newcomer. It wasn't until we arrived that I realised how covered up we always were – there was no way I could have got a tan!

One of the sensible things that I did pack was an enormous supply of 'blueys': the thin, blue airmail letters that you can send via military mail when serving abroad.

Back then, there wasn't wireless Internet in the camps and you had to queue for at least an hour to get onto one of the two computers we had. Even when it was finally your turn, you were only allowed a 20-minute slot. That was it – the PCs were timed, like an Internet café, and would just log you out once your time was up. People weren't using Facebook or Twitter at that time, we weren't allowed mobile phones, and the phone cards we had for calling a landline gave us 10 minutes each week. I'd make a call, say: 'I'm fine, I'm fine – I hope you're well. A bluey's on the way,' and hang up, then call the next person so I was left to keep in touch with everyone I cared about with individual letters. Other things I managed to slip in the box with the cosmetics and the blueys were some comfortable tracksuits for while we were in our tent, my pyjamas to sleep in and some photographs of my friends and family.

I turned 18 on 29 March 2005 and left for Iraq two days later. You're not given a talk of doom or asked to write letters for your loved ones, like in the movies, but I found thoughts about the seriousness of the situation fluttering into my mind whenever I was doing the most boring jobs imaginable. I'd be washing up, or loading shopping into the back of my car, and suddenly I'd think, 'This is stern stuff, I really am off to Iraq'.

As I said goodbye to my friends and family, the fact that it might be for the last time flickered across my mind. I pushed it away as fast as I could, determined to cherish the final hug with my mum.

The nerves finally kicked in on the plane out there. For all my talk of being a tomboy, going off to the BRIT School under my own steam and then getting through the selection and military training, I had never actually been that far from home before. I had always stayed relatively close to my Home Counties roots and had never had to confront, let alone work, in an entirely different culture. The hours that we spent travelling only emphasised the enormous distance; this was more than going on exercise – it was the real thing. Fidgety and sweaty, I was pretty much unable to talk sense to anyone around me on the flight; I just tried to keep myself to myself and not let it show too much. I'm sure the others were the same as the plane quickly divided into those who were very chatty and the ones who were almost silent.

We flew from RAF Brize Norton to Basra. As we came in to land, we had to put on our helmets, shut all of the windows and turn all of the lights off so that no one below saw us land. Then we got a helicopter up to our base. Army helicopters are not the small nifty ones, the sort that you see millionaires and celebrities landing in at stately homes; they are large military vehicles that soldiers run onto, wearing their helmets and rucksacks. There's no luxurious seating designed to show off the views either. We sit in rows, facing each other in the unembellished metal interior. The military helicopters look like the ones that crop up at the end of James Bond movies, when the baddie ends up hanging out the back: stark, utilitarian and really uncomfortable. They are all about getting cargo from one location to the next and on this occasion, we were the cargo.

The realisation that I truly was in Iraq didn't hit me until we caught the coaches that were waiting for us as we disembarked the helicopter. We had landed during the night and as we trundled towards the base, there were tanks on either side of the armed coaches. I fell asleep in my seat with my helmet on and woke up with a jolt when the coach stopped. As I stepped off the vehicle, the heat blasted me in the face, almost stopping me from inhaling. It was like the sensation you get when you land on holiday and step off the plane onto the steps. Whooosh! A hairdryer of holiday air blows you in the face and you get a thrill, knowing you'll be on the beach before too long. Only this time I was blasted in the face with sand, while knowing there was no beach anywhere near. My sleep had left me disorientated and I had no idea where I actually was: on the street, in a city, in the desert or on a camp? I was utterly confused. Around me, everything was unfamiliar – not just the darkness and the heat, but every smell, every sound, every sensation. I had never felt so far from home.

'Welcome to Iraq,' I thought to myself.

The first two weeks there, we were not given official roles as we were still acclimatising. To make sure we were coping with the heat, we did a lot of physical training: we needed it. I have always prided myself on aiming to be as well prepared as possible for any given situation and on trying my hardest, but I was left embarrassed when I let myself down on the very first day. I passed out in the sun. Heat is something you can't negotiate with; it was something I couldn't get around by working hard or being thorough. My body simply let me down, for the first time in my life – I'm sure the nerves and emotion I'd been feeling had something to do with it too.

We were lined up outside, being given a talk from a senior soldier about protocol on the camp. We were new but keen to show that we were up to the job, there to make a difference. I could feel the sweat trickling down the small of my back and gathering along my hairline. My fingers started to tingle, my vision blurred and BAM! Suddenly my legs went from beneath me and I crumpled to the floor in front of the whole regiment. I could imagine what people would be thinking for the rest of the tour of duty: there's that girl, the weak one, the one who couldn't cope. My cheeks were pretty hot when I came to, but they were burning with shame as well. For a while, I tried to keep a low profile until I got my confidence back and people had moved on to the next gossip, but it didn't help me settle in.

For the first few months I was very homesick and even though I had wanted so badly to prove myself, I did not enjoy the experience of being on tour at all. The process of settling in took much longer than the two-week official acclimatisation that was allocated. Usually if you're abroad somewhere very hot, you can put on a little floaty sundress but you can't do that on duty: we were wearing our uniforms and carrying all our kit, too. It wasn't just the heat, though – there was the constant dustiness and the ever-pervading smell of badly constructed drains and litter that hadn't been properly disposed of. There were rotting animal carcasses and open drains along the roadsides, which meant that even if the heat and the dust weren't getting to you too much, the less-than-fragrant air usually would. On top of all that, I missed my family and friends more than I had imagined possible.

On week three, we moved to our permanent eight-man tents in the desert. It was only then that our packed box of personal belongings arrived in the freight containers. They had been shipped out, which explained why they had taken so long to arrive. We were all abuzz with excitement when we went down in numbered groups to collect our labelled boxes. Though it looked like one of thousands in that container, it meant the world to me when I eventually got my hands on mine. I was thrilled to see my photographs and home comforts again, although all that fake tan now seemed so incongruous. What was I thinking? We were living in tents and the shower blocks – I mean, 'luxurious spa facilities' – were just Portakabins.

The only gender difference between the 'spa area' on camp was the men had four Portakabins while the women had two as there were fewer of us. Otherwise, all the amenities were the same: glamorous wafts of dust and sand, as well as a blast of hot sticky heat were provided for all of us whenever we exited the shower area, meaning that we remained almost as filthy as when we entered. As a result, there really was no point at all in trying to look nice, let alone attempting to apply fake tan with all that generously supplied grit flying around! I rolled my eyes and thought to myself how long it seemed since the day that I packed.

A week later, Stacey was moved to another camp, leaving me alone and feeling rather vulnerable. At first, I was unhappy but I had no choice but to start making new friends. I can see now that it was probably a good thing in the end, although one of my most bone-chilling moments in Iraq happened shortly after she left.

I was quite paranoid about being alone with so many people I didn't know in such a foreign environment, but generally I had been sleeping well. One night, however, I went to bed only to wake with a start a couple of hours later as someone had just grabbed me. Oh my God, I thought. Who is that? I turned on the bedside lamp as fast as I could. There was a mosquito net over me, but I peered through it to try and catch sight of whoever it was: I couldn't see anything. Slowly, quietly, I unzipped the mosquito net and eased my head under the small, fold-up bed that I was lying on, in order to check underneath it: nothing.

I turned the bedside light off, but stayed sitting up in bed, terrified, wondering what to do next. As I sat there, I started to hear whispering voices. My blood ran cold: I could hear the others in the tent snoozing gently but the urgent-sounding whispers grew ever louder.

I was terrified. Of course, this was a situation that would be scary wherever you were, but I was aware that we were in a warzone and whatever I did next could have an effect on my colleagues as well as myself. I stayed still, waiting to see if anyone moved, but I must have dozed off as moments later, I could feel someone tapping my shoulder as if to wake me up. Again, I turned the light on. The voices grew louder, although I couldn't catch any of the actual words that were being said. Slowly, carefully, I crept out of bed and left the tent: this was a situation I had to report.

I put on my combat boots and started to prowl around the camp, checking every entrance and exit that I could find. Eventually, I got down to the front of the camp, where someone was on guard. It was a lad I had got to know called Lance. I was shaking with fear and must have looked bonkers in my combat boots and homely pyjamas.

'Kat, what on earth are you doing?' he asked.

'There are people in my tent, whispering,' I told him, wide-eyed with fear. I'm sure he thought I was nuts.

'Can't you tell them to be quiet?'

'No, it's not the guys in the tent, it's someone else. There are intruders in my tent. One of them deliberately woke me up.'

'What do you mean?'

'Someone's in my tent, whispering. And another jolted me awake.'

'But I've been on guard and no one has gone in there.'

'I swear, there's someone in there. Please, find out what's going on. The others are at risk.'

'Let's go and check.'

Lance came with me and we checked the tent again. There was no one there but my sleeping colleagues. I could still hear the whispering and I was becoming more and more agitated.

'Can't you hear them? Can't you hear them?' I kept on saying, grabbing his arm.

'No, Kat, there's no one here,' Lance did his best to reassure me.

I remained unconvinced. In the end I became so distraught that Lance had to come off guard and spend the rest of the night sitting in the TV room with me. The guard commander had guessed what my problem was: before leaving for Iraq, we had been prescribed anti-malaria tablets. I'd never taken them before, so I didn't know you can have hallucinations because of them – you just don't imagine it will ever happen to you. The guard commander tried to explain it to me there and then, but I was in such a state and I only became more upset that no one else could hear the voices. It was the most scared I have ever been in my life: I even felt cold – I was shivering with terror, despite being in the desert. For the rest of the night, I sat there watching the Cartoon Channel with Lance, shaking like a leaf, determined not to sleep in case the whispering got louder. Lance was great – I think he was a bit freaked out but he was really sympathetic.

The next morning I was taken to the doctor's and told that I had been suffering from hallucinations, not the sinister voices of an unseen enemy. Apparently it is relatively common, so I was immediately taken off the anti-malaria tablets and given the next day off to sleep. Within a few hours the whispering stopped and I was back to normal, but I will never forget the fear or disorientation that I experienced.

The camp itself was like a mini-city; it took 15 or 20 minutes to walk from one end to the other. Its official name was Shabai Log base, but we called it Shibiza because it was always so hot there. Yeah, it's a pretty rubbish nickname but when you're in the desert, you'll do almost anything to make each other laugh!

Stationed there were a mixture of Forces from all over the world, with British shops (the NAAFI) and American ones, such as the PX; also restaurants and bars, which meant that we didn't always have to eat the military food provided. There was a lot of roast meat as part of the Army food and after a while, I just couldn't handle it every night. After a day of working hard in the dust and heat, I couldn't face the kind of dinner that is designed to warm you up in the pub on a chilly Sunday lunchtime.

As a result, almost every evening I would walk to Pizza Hut for dinner. I preferred the food, but also it felt like a little bit of 'me' time; some civilisation after living and working in the same area as all of my direct colleagues, who were mostly greedy men. It felt like I was off out for the night, even though in reality, I was still contained in 'Shibiza Town'. That pizza place and the milkshake bar nearby became real retreats for me, and I got to know all the staff, who were locals. It was a big deal for them to be working on the camp – it was a security risk for them to take, as some Iraqis considered it disloyal for them to be working for us. On the other hand, they had to go through huge security checks every time they entered camp to make sure that they were not acting undercover in any way. It was good money for them, though, and I never met a single one who seemed in any way dishonourable.

By the end of the tour, I felt like a little part of their family and on my last night there, the staff had even bought me a traditional silver necklace to say that I was the best customer that they had ever had! I missed them on my first night home from Iraq, when my mum rubbed her hands together and grinned at me: 'Let's get you some proper food for once – I'm going to sort you out with a nice traditional Sunday roast.' She was convinced that this was a treat I had been dreaming of for months: if only she'd known!

We had evenings off to chill and watch TV in the TV tent – we could watch the news and programmes like *Hollyoaks*, although the episodes were about three weeks behind the UK. And we'd chat and play board games like chess, or made-up guessing games. Sometimes we were on guard at night, too.

About four or five weeks into the tour I was finally

allowed off camp. For the first time, I would be part of the Commanding Officer's rover group. The commanding officer is the big boss, the man at the top of the food chain: the head of a regiment of about 2,000 people. The civilian equivalent is probably a regional manager. Being part of his rover group meant operating as his security – going where he was going, which was usually to a nearby town or village for a meeting with a mayor or a tribal dignitary. Our job was to protect him by riding in armoured vehicles before and after him, keeping an eye out for anything suspicious in the surrounding area. It might be armed figures at windows, suspicious packages on the side of the road or anything that could pose a threat. I was very excited to be getting a taste of the action at last, but also nervous to be leaving the confines of the camp, which I had only just got used to.

We were travelling in vehicles called Snatches. These are armoured Land Rovers and they are used for patrolling areas of low risk. You've probably seen them on the news. They have a driver, someone on top looking out and maybe a couple of people down in the vehicle itself. I was riding on top, in the observation role. As we approached the edge of the Shabai Log camp, I realised how enormous it was: 20 miles long, filled with row upon row of tents and Portakabins. We came to the edge of the camp, ringed with fences and with several posts, where people were keeping watch, but we were in the middle of nowhere. I had imagined we would be on the suburb of a town or city, but really, we were in the middle of the desert. There was a good reason for this, though: you could see anyone approaching from miles away.

For me, hanging out of the vehicles on the top was one of the best feelings in the world and the first day that I did it, it was unbelievable. I felt a rush of adrenaline coursing through me. The air was so hot, it was good to feel a bit of breeze on my face, but mostly I felt a real sensation of, 'Here I am, this is what I trained to do, and I'm doing it!' I must have had a huge grin on my face: I felt like a dog who had been allowed to stick his head out of the car window, but I made sure not to reveal how thrilled I was. It was work, after all.

It took about an hour to get to the town we were visiting and as we approached the outskirts, suddenly I felt the nerves creeping up again. On the street, people were waving towards us and our vehicle. At that moment Iraqis stopped being anonymous faces from the news: I had a proper sense of a country filled with individuals. I could hear their voices, I could smell their clothes, I could see them interacting with each other; this wasn't play-acting any more. Those were people's lives and my behaviour could have a huge effect on them. The houses we were passing surprised me – just four mud walls, with large families living in them. I had never seen anything like it before, nor had I seen women in burqas. Roads were just dirt tracks, with dead animals piled up to the sides and children playing nearby in bare feet. The poverty of the country and the way that the people had been treated was brought to life in front of me like never before. I was so busy looking at my surroundings that I did not realise anyone was looking at me, but I soon found out how wrong I was.

When the vehicles stopped and we got out, several men immediately rushed over to stare at me. Although I had my helmet on, I still had my long blonde plait running down my back: I could feel their eyes on me, but they were largely quiet. I helped my crew check the surrounding area to make sure it was secure for the commanding officer and once that was done, we were allowed to take our helmets off in order to look less threatening to the locals.

Quickly, lots of old men and children gathered round me and started touching my hair and head. Apparently my blondeness was very rare and so few of them had ever seen anything like it. It was also seen as a sign of luck. I could not communicate with them because of the language barrier and I was also carrying my weapon, which made me nervous as they were getting so close to it. Being in a warzone with people wanting to touch your head is very frightening, but at the same time I was out there in a peacekeeping role, trying to train then so I didn't want to show fear. We weren't fighting, we were trying to help. But a crowd of strangers was still touching me. Before long, I felt completely overwhelmed and could sense the panic bubbling up inside me.

Seeing this, one of the lads from the tank grabbed me

and shoved me back in the vehicle. 'You'll get used to it,' he said, as we drove away. But I wasn't sure that I would: what with the fainting, the hallucinations and Stacey having been moved to another camp, I was starting to feel as everything was getting on top of me before I had even begun to do anything useful.

The day ended on a high, though. Later on, we stopped at Basra Palace camp, where Stacey was now stationed. I wanted to see my mate and tell her everything, and was thrilled when I found her, even if I was insanely jealous that she was sleeping in bunk beds in an old palace instead of in the tents I was in. Compared to my accommodation, this was luxury – and her food was delicious, too. It's amazing how different a meal can taste if it's been cooked in an old palace, not a dusty tent. Boosted by dinner and good chat with my bezzie, I felt determined not to let the initial acclimatisation problems hold me back in Iraq.

On the way home, we stopped for the team to make sure an area was secure. We exited the vehicle to check for explosive devices and very soon the same thing happened with my hair. This time I took a deep breath, and attempted to deal with the situation better. I smiled and gestured to people that they needed to keep their distance. They seemed to understand – a breakthrough! I had learned what it is possible to express to people, even if you don't speak their language. Presenting yourself as confident and in control of the situation isn't just a verbal skill, it's how you hold yourself and approach a group.

When I got home, I was buzzing and I felt safer and more in control from that day onwards.

Before long I started to make new friends and then I really began to appreciate being in Iraq. I was getting to see a culture and a country that others might never have the opportunity to experience. It was obviously very daunting as an 18-year-old, but soon I was thriving on it. The patriotism and pride that I have in the Army had never dawned on me when I joined or while I was in training – that was no part of it. It was only when I got to Iraq that I really saw what a value there was in what we were doing and what a great job, full of opportunities, I had. More and more, I also started to appreciate what I had back home as I witnessed the poverty out there.

The people I met were incredible. When you leave for a warzone you imagine that everyone there is going to be out to get you, but quickly it became clear that most people were simply trying to get on with their lives. A lot of the time, they knew less about what was going on in their own country than people in Europe did. And most of the country was happy that we were there, helping them out.

If people had asked me two years earlier if I'd be happy being woken at 4am in the middle of the desert to get up for an uncomfortable two-hour drive and then a hard day's work, I would have laughed in their face.

'No way, mate! I'll be on stage or recording my debut album,' might have been my response. But I felt alive and excited by the tasks I was undertaking and the goals that I was achieving.

My main role in Iraq was as a 'female searcher'. This meant that when intelligence was received that there might be a threat to security somewhere, it was our task to simply go and show our presence, or go and actively search a building and its inhabitants for weapons or explosives. It was British Army policy for there to be females on each search team in case women or children under the age of 13 were on the premises (they could only be searched by female military personnel, such as myself). Sometimes we would hear there was a rocket device at a location that could be used to blow up helicopters in mid-air and we would have to go and search for it. On other occasions we wouldn't be searching for a rocket device itself but simply something that could be used to set off the notorious Improvised Explosive Device (IED) roadside bombs. This could be anything electrical, such as a mobile phone. Sometimes, these bombs were hidden in animal carcasses on the side of the road and then set off remotely, killing the troops who were patrolling and searching the area. It was one thing to kill soldiers, but sometimes children were killed too.

We were never told what time of day or night it might be, or who we'd be going with, but about once a week we would suddenly be sent without notice into people's houses to make these checks. The timings always varied, as it was vital that no one ever spotted a routine to our searches.

One week there would be three searches at night or in the very early morning to ensure an element of surprise. Other times, there would be a week of quiet. The trouble was, the timings were also a surprise to us, sometimes while we were snoozing away: we had to be up and out within minutes, regardless of how long we would be gone.

As I soon found out, some searches were just for an hour or two – there and back. But the operations being performed were very varied and on other occasions, we were gone for as long as a week. Being pretty much at the bottom of the food chain, I wasn't always informed what the intelligence or the reason for the operation was: we were just told what we were to do and expected to carry out our orders.

At first, it felt very intrusive to go into people's homes and wake them up to search their beds, their clothes, even their hair. I had real compassion for them and to begin with, I felt uncomfortable and domineering. But it didn't take long for me to realise that we were rarely searching places without good reason and that the meek-looking Iraqi women could sometimes be holding secrets just as much as the aggressive-seeming men. Usually, we would find things in the building itself, but I also discovered batteries and wires in women's hair on occasions as well as mobile phones – all essentials used to detonate bombs. Some of these things looked so irrelevant and tatty but if we hadn't found them, they could have been responsible for taking the lives of many.

I didn't see everyone I came across as the enemy, though – and they weren't. In my day-to-day interaction, I loved meeting the Muslim women out there and always had plenty to chat to them about. We had interpreters with us all the time, but I managed to learn some Arabic (I'm still not brilliant) and it was amazing, getting to know them, too. I was often intrigued to see how fancy their clothes were under their burqas. That scene in *Sex and the City 2* is no joke: I came across some serious designer threads under there when I was searching ladies in some of the bigger, more affluent houses. At first, I was gobsmacked. On the whole, I felt very sorry for them for having to wear what were effectively two outfits in that heat, though.

In turn, they were intrigued to see a woman doing a job like mine, as they don't work at all. They didn't seem to be judging me, or to feel sympathy for the fact that I 'had to' work, but they were intrigued by how we had a culture where I was able to do this. My independence appeared to inspire awe and curiosity more than anything else. They never seemed to think, 'What's she playing at?' but often asked 'Why? Why are you working with the men?' They were largely very supportive towards us, but seemed baffled when I explained that it was because I had chosen to do so. This made me realise how lucky I am and how many opportunities I have – it really is two different worlds.

I also got to know a group of Iraqi kids as part of my patrols. Often they spoke more English than the adults, picked up from cartoons and pop songs. So while I was out on patrols, I'd sometimes hear a scuffle of feet followed by: 'Lady play! Please play, lady!' or 'Give me water, lady! Lady, lady, water!' Or even sometimes: 'Lady, give me gun?' Er, *no*, that would definitely be a step too far! I'd see them pretty much every day, be high-fiving them and chatting to them and giving them water in the street, and then at the end of my six months one of them bought me a necklace with a 'K' on it. I was so touched.

I was surprised by how big the difference between the rich and the poor was, too. Some families lived between nothing more than mud walls, with 20 people in a room: men, women and children, all shoved together. Then you'd see another house close by, with marble walls and gold toilets. There was no difference in importance to us, but it seemed like a different world. If anything, it was usually the richer ones who were the more dangerous.

With a job where you basically have to demand to go into people's homes all the time, you need to have a certain personality and approach and I tried to be very sensitive to that. You had to be cooperative but as I learned, you could never entirely let your guard down, as danger was never that far away.

In the September of my tour, in 2005, I was involved in a search operation that put me in the greatest danger I had ever been in. We went to search someone's house and on this occasion, one of my colleagues found something specific that raised a potential threat. I cannot elaborate on what it was, as we are not allowed to go into details of a particular operation, but the threat was significant enough that our sergeant decided we had to detain the person and take him back for questioning. In this instance, it was important not to behave like an aggressor but to say that to be clear, we needed to talk with him.

'We've got someone,' one of my colleagues told me. 'He's coming back in our vehicle.' The man was immediately taken away.

We got back into the vehicle. There were two people up on top, including my sergeant, and I was down inside the vehicle with the detainee and a second soldier, while the driver was at the front. The man we had detained was in his forties or fifties. He was of a large build, with a moustache and beard. He was certainly a threatening presence, especially as he was staring at me intently. I stared back in the darkness, trying to show that he didn't intimidate me. If I had just gazed into my lap sheepishly then he would have immediately taken control of the atmosphere so I made sure to meet his gaze.

For around 25 minutes we travelled like this: part of a larger convoy of vehicles, just staring each other out. Suddenly, the vehicle just seemed to go from under us. What the hell was going on? Is this what it feels like to be blown up? I wondered. The vehicle started to turn over and from above, I could hear my female sergeant screaming. It was actually only a road traffic accident – our tank had swerved to avoid a bump in the road and rolled off from the raised mound that we were driving along. As part of the fall, the vehicle rolled over three times: with the dark metallic belly of the vehicle we were rattling around, being thrown from one end to the other, hitting the metal walls, floors and seating.

When I came round, it was pitch-black and I could hear my colleagues screaming above me. They weren't screaming words at each other, simply yelling in agony, though. The lad next to me – a fellow soldier – was completely dazed, just staring blankly and I could hear the driver yelling from the front to check that we were all OK. Everything seemed to have happened so fast, I still didn't understand what was going on. A chink of light started to come in from outside and as soon as I could, I looked around to find out where the detainee was.

What I managed to see was that the Iraqi had two weapons. One of them was my own rifle, which had come off during the roll from the accident. I knew that they were loaded weapons, made ready to shoot, with 30 rounds of ammunition in them, even if he didn't. But by the look on his face, I imagined that he knew exactly what was going on and that all he had to do was pull the trigger – after all, he was pointing it at me and one of the lads. Bloodcurdling screams were still coming from above; it turned out that some of the team had dislocated arms and broken legs.

Physically, I seemed to be OK but I was still in shock, trying to work out what sounds were coming from where, what was an immediate threat and what was just panic.

One realisation crept its icy way into my mind, though: I was probably about to die. The fact that a man was holding a gun in my face seemed to make this pretty definite. Initially, I felt resigned to it and so I decided my priority was to do what I could do to help so that my death wasn't entirely pointless. But what had felt like resignation turned out to be a fleeting thought: at that moment a survival instinct I never knew I had kicked in. There was no way that I was prepared to die yet, let alone like this. It hit me in the eyes: do or die time, I *had* to do something. I tried not to panic, even though I was looking down the barrel of a rifle – *my* rifle.

Somehow instinct took hold and the fighter that I had trained to be emerged: with every ounce of strength I possessed, I made a fist and punched him square in the face. I gasped when I heard the massive cracking noise it made. Oh my God, I've just punched someone in the face, I found myself thinking – I think we were both as shocked as each other by the force of my blow. He dropped the guns; I leaped forward and quickly grabbed both weapons. At that moment someone came to the back of the vehicle and opened the door to see what was going on inside.

As quickly as possible I scrambled out of the back and helped the others to make sure that the detainee was back under proper control. We clambered up the mound again to reach the other vehicles in the convoy, one of which I sat in the back of. Our vehicle was left behind and the detainee kept with us. We started moving again and after a couple of minutes, one of the guys from that team looked at me and asked: 'Why have you got two weapons?' I explained what had just happened, not quite believing it myself. He shouted to the Sergeant Major and told him the story. No one had realised what a lucky escape we had all just had, even me. Suddenly I felt more scared than I had when it was actually happening.

It was only then that the pain hit me and I realised that I had been limping as I'd clambered from the accident. I was rushed back to the medical centre on camp, still in shock. After a few hours it came to light that I had very serious whiplash. My neck was totally crooked, my ear almost touching my shoulder. Slowly, the others from the accident started to arrive. One of the lads' shoulders was so badly dislocated that he was on a morphine drip and my sergeant had unbelievably bad bruising flowering up all over her body from rolling over and over her weapon in the accident. Bizarrely, it was shaped exactly like a rifle in the spot of soft flesh on her body so it looked like a transfer or tattoo.

Unbelievably, at this moment I spotted the Iraqi detainee being guided past me, under arrest. He was complaining that he had a bruised hip and shouting at us for injuring him. Of course he had a right to be medically checked, but as he had been moments from shooting me in the face, I found it more than difficult to summon up any sympathy for him.

By the time I was allowed to head back to my tent for a

rest it was morning and my colleagues were up and about. When some of my friends saw me, they rushed up to me in a huge panic. Word had spread that there had been an accident but no one knew what type or what had happened. The reason they were so worried was because when people die in Iraq, or Afghanistan now, the rest of us don't always hear immediately that there has been a fatality. All we are told is that there has been an accident, until events can be confirmed. When my bed stayed empty all night and the hubbub in the medical centre was becoming noticeable, my pals had started to think the worst.

By then, I was so exhausted and the pain was spreading throughout my battered and bruised body, not to mention the shock. I just told them the basics and left out anything to do with my confrontation with the Iraqi detainee.

'I'm OK, we're all back – I just need to sleep,' was all I could manage as they huddled round, brimming with questions. Once I hit my bed, I just passed out and didn't wake up until the next morning, some 24 hours later. When I saw my friends again, they had been told the full story and were filled with praise and admiration.

After that incident I was nervous about rolling in the Snatch vehicle again, but I managed to block out the memory of the Iraqi detainee himself. I didn't even want to remember what he looked like, as I couldn't have him turning up in my subconscious when I had an important job to do. My ability to focus and be a good soldier was the priority and I decided that forgetting all about him was the quickest way to stop him from having any power over me. Remembering the incident and the man's face staring me out at close range, my gun raised towards my head, still has the power to upset me. But back then, there was no time to dwell on it: I had to get on with my job.

Whatever you might think about my bravery on that occasion, there is something I would really beg everyone to remember: I was not alone in showing any courage. Back in 2005, people were dying in Iraq, every month. Soldiers were performing acts of amazing bravery on a daily basis. What happened to me is interesting to journalists now because I'm a beauty queen, but at the time my attitude was: 'I'm not dead; therefore I am one of the lucky ones. I owe it to the others to keep going.'

I am really proud to tell this story, and I'm always happy to talk to the media about it when they have shown an interest. Since 2005, I must have discussed it hundreds of times. A big deal has been made about my actions because I am female, but it really shouldn't have been. Women *are* brave – I see that every day in all walks of life.

This is my definitive memory of what happened then; from now on, I'm going to try and stop telling the story. There are other soldiers out there who have done incredibly heroic things: they have lost limbs saving the lives of others and they have sacrificed their lives in trying to protect the security of this country. Some are women, some are men, and very few of them are ever celebrated or ever mentioned in the media. I have had a great opportunity to tell my story but I hope that when people hear my account, they will remember that I'm just one of many. When I tell you what went on in Iraq, I represent thousands of brave and committed people.

CHAPTER FOUR

HOME AGAIN – ENGLAND AND MISS ENGLAND

YOU KNOW the feeling when you step off the plane after a sunny holiday and feel crisp, damp British air on your face? It's a funny combination of sadness that you can no longer guarantee you'll feel warm in just a T-shirt all day combined with relief that you don't have to worry about sweating and sun cream any more. Most of all, you feel as if you're at home.

Well, I felt that to the power of one hundred the day that I stepped off the final flight home from Iraq in November 2005. Back then, the Forces' return home had not yet been embraced by the communities close to the Air Force bases with ceremonies such as the ones at Wootton Bassett; the number of deaths was not necessarily lower, but the public commitment to honouring them definitely was. The feeling of joy to be home was no less intense, however. I hugged myself with happiness as we rode the coach from RAF Brize Norton, where we had landed, back to camp.

That doesn't mean I hadn't enjoyed the tour of duty in Iraq: quite the opposite. I nearly missed my flight – I was still so busy by the time it finally ended. Just as the first three months had crawled by, the final three whizzed past so quickly that it feels like a blur. As the return date rushed towards me, faster and faster, I could barely remember how lonely and unhappy I had been at first. I was sad to say goodbye to good old Shibiza as the tour had been such an important experience for me, but I was equally thrilled to be home.

It took three days of travelling to reach base and when we did, we had two sets of unpacking to do. Obviously we had to unpack the belongings we had brought back with us, but we also had to unpack the kit we *hadn't* taken to Iraq. Before we departed, we'd had to pack up our personal belongings. This was so that our belongings could all be stored in a safe place in case anything happened to us while we were on tour and our things needed to be returned to our loved ones. It might sound a bit morbid, but it is actually standard procedure.

Opening up the boxes of belongings that I hadn't seen for six months was an emotional experience. I remember getting out of the shower on that first night back and just sitting on the end of the bed in my pyjamas. Although I was in an exhausted daze, seeing those boxes really reminded me of just how lucky I was that I had made it back safely, and I spent a few minutes thinking about how many didn't. I had become so used to living out of one bag, I couldn't believe how much stuff I had! And the girly side of me was thrilled to discover that lots of it didn't fit any more as I had lost quite a bit of weight, thanks to my hectic lifestyle. I'm usually around nine stone but I'd gone down to a size six.

We spent the weekend reacclimatising at camp: there were various medical tests and talks that we all had to go through before we were fully checked off and allowed home for some rest. I was utterly drained by the time I finally reached my mum's house – my parents divorced when I was about 16 – and dreaming of sleeping in a comfy bed. There were nights in Iraq when I lay on my camp bed, thinking about how cosy it would be to be back under the family roof, in a lovely clean room, pulling a fluffy duvet round me for warmth. Bliss! Months in a sandy tent really taught me what I loved about the UK… and beds were a big part of it.

I was so exhausted on my return that I actually felt a bit smothered by the number of people who wanted to come over and say hi and see photographs. There seemed to be a never-ending parade of well-wishers. I hadn't realised it at the time, but I had become very used to seeing a select, regular group of people. When I was on camp, I felt entirely safe because I knew that security was so high but off camp, I always had so much adrenaline coursing through my veins that I was on high alert. It's hard to relax when you're in a tank, wearing a helmet, but it does give you a sense that there are protective layers around you. Back in England, though, I found myself a bit flustered by being on a busy high street: I wasn't used to it. The extremes of a secure camp and a dangerous town were nothing like the sense of keeping an eye on your bag while you're in a busy Saturday shopping centre. I felt confused, coming from somewhere so dangerous and yet feeling vulnerable on my own doorstep.

Given what I'd been through, it was very odd that – if anything – I felt less safe when I got home. It was the sudden change in environment that was a shock to the system but the stream of visitors helped me to get used to normality pretty quickly and before long, I had my confidence back up. It was also a relief to realise that finally, my family was taking my career seriously: I had proved conclusively that I was in the Army and doing it properly; no one could argue with that now.

Despite the reassurances and compliments that my friends and family showered me with on my return, I never mentioned the confrontation that I had had with the Iraqi who took my weapon. So much else had changed, so much time had passed, and I had so many photographs of me doing other things that I just didn't think of it. The details of the event got lost in the rest of the 'Welcome Home' celebrations. 'Why bother to bring up the bad stuff when I could show them the photographs that Stacey and I had taken specifically to entertain them with?' I thought to myself. After all, when Stacey and I had only been in Iraq for a couple of weeks – before we had even left the camp – we had taken lots of photos of ourselves in 'tough' Army poses. Obviously we had been reduced to giggles within minutes of trying, especially as we were just on camp, standing near a dusty wall, not looking very impressive at all but I was glad to have something to show the parade of visitors once I got home.

My inadvertent secret didn't last for long because once our two weeks' leave was finished, at the end of November, we had the medal parade for our tour of duty. I hadn't actually invited any of my family as I thought they wouldn't be that interested; how wrong I was.

The parade took place on the main drill square at our Pirbright Barracks, a large tarmac area in the centre of all the main buildings, used for both exercise and parades. All 1,000 of us were there, standing proud in our desert combat uniform, thrilled to have done our duty and returned home. The important thing for our regiment was that we had all returned safely. I appreciate that fact all the more now as the Royal Anglian Regiment has been to Afghanistan since and lost eight lives.

The senior officer who was visiting to award us our medals read out each of our names. I don't know how the organisers arranged this, but each medal had our name and rank on it, and as the officer walked along the ranks, we were congratulated and presented with an individual medal. I was thrilled to be receiving an award to show that

I had done something of real value for the Armed Forces. These days I keep my medal in a box in my bedroom and only put it on whenever we wear our best uniform.

It was a bright, sunny winter's day and the parade was a lengthy process to ensure each of us had our moment. It is surprisingly difficult to stay alert while standing smartly in front of so many people, so by the time the officer got to the commendations section of the ceremony, I was starting to daydream a little. My mind was wandering as I felt the sun on my back and the officer began reading the citations – the description of what each soldier has done to deserve the specific commendation.

Hmmm, that's impressive, I'd thought, when I heard the first one. I had no idea that he had done that – I think I shared a vehicle with him a few times.

After the citation had been read out, the soldier broke rank and marched out towards the officer to collect his commendation. While the second commendation was given out, I found my mind returning to my own time in Iraq and then what I'd be doing at the weekend. I still had a few friends I had yet to catch up with properly and some Christmas presents to buy.

While I was in my mild daydream, I heard the name 'Hodge', but didn't think anything of it. After all, there were a few Hodges in the regiment, and a Hodgson, so I didn't think for a minute that it would be my name that had been called. Suddenly I felt a hand flicking mine. I turned slightly and frowned at the soldier standing next to me.

'It's you,' he whispered from the side of his mouth. 'March out!'

I looked around me. What was going on? I snapped to and realised that it was my name being called out. But what was I supposed to be marching out for? I stepped forward and started marching. It was as if I was moving through honey.

Where am I going? What am I going up there for? Please tell me it really is my name that they read out... I am going to look so stupid otherwise.

Suddenly, the officer's voice sounded echoing and far away, as if he was underwater. But as I got my bearings I realised what he was reading out: by the time that I reached the officer at the front of the parade square, I knew that I was being awarded a commendation for bravery during the incident recovering our weapons from the Iraqi detainee.

I was presented with my commendation, which is an enormous scroll detailing the event, encased in an official frame. The officers gathered at the front of the square all shook my hand and congratulated me.

As I marched back to my original position in the parade ground, I felt myself glowing with pride and beamed when I saw my various friends grinning from their positions within the rows. I had to struggle to keep my face as serious and official as possible, and so did they. It was a moment of huge pride, but not without sadness too: I was painfully aware that many others complete acts just as brave but that there were, and continue to be, many who never return from a tour of duty. I just did what any soldier would have done in that situation: to award me is to award all of us.

Once we were off the parade square and standing at ease my sergeant major came over to me.

'Excuse me, Corporal Hodge,' he said. 'BBC News are here, and they would like to speak to you.'

'To *me*? – What for?'

'They would like to interview you about your commendation.'

It was the first time that I had ever been approached by the media; already I was in a real daze about the commendation and the memories of Iraq – I could barely speak. But before I knew it, a local reporter was in front of me with a microphone. He was a classic local news guy, with a moustache and wearing a raincoat despite the sunny weather.

'How does it feel to have been awarded a commendation? I understand it was only one of three, and you were the only woman,' he asked.

'I don't really know,' I replied. 'I'm still getting used to it. I certainly wasn't expecting it.'

The BBC still use that clip of me today, whenever there is any Miss England news: me with my old blonde hair marching out towards the officer, trying very hard to hide my combination of confusion and pride. Almost immediately afterwards, a local reporter from a Tunbridge

Wells paper asked to get a photograph of me in my uniform as well.

The rest of the day went in a blur. I called my mum straightaway and she sounded pleased for me, but seemed to think it was just some sort of internal pat on the back from the local bosses. The fact that I hadn't considered the parade worth inviting her to meant that she didn't realise the importance of the honour until she saw her daughter on the news! I spent the afternoon in the bar on camp, with friends and colleagues coming up to congratulate me and saying they had no idea what I had done. Why would they? I hadn't bothered to tell anyone. I kept reassuring them that it was no big secret, simply not something I chose to show off about.

That weekend I realised there was no hiding the event, though. I had gone home for my old friend Leonie's birthday and we were hanging out in a local café, having a proper hangover breakfast, flicking through the papers.

'*Whoa!*' she shrieked, putting down her cutlery.

'Ooh what?' I asked, expecting a nice juicy nugget of celebrity gossip.

'It's *you!*'

And so it was. As Leonie held up the paper, I saw my own face staring back at me. The photograph that the local photographer had taken was there with a report on my commendation. That photo was in most of the papers and there was even a cartoon of me in the *Sun*: it showed a pile of punched Iraqis around me, while I was standing above them, saying: 'Oh no, that's done it. You've broken a nail!' I loved the idea that they had seen me as a tough girl and a girly girl – exactly what I felt I was. If only they had known what was coming next, and if only I'd known it wouldn't be the last time I'd be featured in the newspaper! As Leonie and I sat there, surveying the papers around me, I remembered the days when I was at the BRIT School, wanting to be famous. I never imagined that I would hit the papers for actually doing something useful.

And the attention didn't stop there: within hours, the Army press office called me with requests for more interviews, including *GMTV* with Lorraine Kelly. I've always loved that show and so I leapt at the chance.

'Ooh, what shall I wear?' was the first thing I thought as I started planning my television début. The answer came back pretty fast: your uniform. Of course, I was going on to represent the Armed Forces so I had to look the part – it was a part of my identity now.

I only realised the full repercussions of looking the part when I got to the studio the next morning. I was allowed to bring a friend, so I had Leonie with me. She spent the night at my house beforehand as a chauffeur-driven car was sent to collect us at 4am. Though bleary-eyed, we were delirious with excitement by the time we arrived at the studio and we loved the showbiz treatment. We were taken to a Green Room, where we could order all sorts of breakfast food. Leonie and I had a couple of bacon rolls and we were then shown to my dressing room, where we sat around wondering what would happen next – it was about three hours before I was due on air.

'Excuse me,' I asked the researcher who popped in to see how we were getting along. 'Is there anything we need to be doing?'

'No, not to worry – we'll be taking you to Hair and Make-up in a while, which usually takes an hour or so,' was the reply.

'Ah...'

'Is there a problem?'

It wasn't really a problem but that was the moment when I realised the obvious: I was in Army uniform, so my hair had to be in a bun and I was not allowed make-up. Not only would my first appearance on national TV be with an entirely bare face, but we had got up at 4am without needing to. The Hair and Make-up teams must have bunked off early that morning!

That didn't ruin the experience, though – far from it. I loved meeting Lorraine Kelly, who was every bit as warm and friendly as I could have hoped. It was so weird, going on set and seeing that the cosy sofas and decorated areas are just a tiny part of what looks like a massive bus garage. There were hundreds of cameramen and lighting crew: at first, I was staring round like a child on a trip to Disneyland.

What I enjoyed most was the respect that everyone there treated me with. I wasn't just a wannabe trying to get a leg up in showbiz, I was there for a reason for which I could hold my head up high and I knew that day that the Army was going to be a huge part of my life forever. It had shown me the strength that I had, the value of being part of a solid team, and what extraordinary things you can achieve when you least expect it.

I spent another year with the Royal Anglian Regiment until the end of 2006 before a posting as part of the Army's recruiting team in a group representing my Corps. Because I'm so chatty, I had a small amount of experience of the media and had also served in a conflict zone, my seniors thought that I might help to encourage other young women to join the Army. I was totally up for it, and had one of the best years of my career so far.

I spent the year travelling up and down the country, going to schools, recruitment fairs and events promoting the Army, while meeting countless girls who were curious about life in the Forces but had only two frames of reference: Hollywood comedies and dated butch stereotypes.

I quickly realised that if I had seen someone from the Army when I was younger then I might have joined up sooner, but because I had never been exposed to an everyday woman serving in the Forces, I didn't even know it was possible until I saw my brother's experience. What must the girls with no older Army siblings be thinking? It didn't take me long to find out, as some of the questions that they found themselves confident enough to ask me were absolutely extraordinary. Some were hilarious, others a bit unnerving. Here is just a small selection of some of them.

'You have really nice long hair. So is it true that you don't have to shave off all of your hair if you are a woman in the Army?' (Yes)

'Is it true that when you go on exercise or to a warzone, the men are given special injections to kill their sex drive, just in case?' (No)

'Would I ever get any time off at weekends or evenings, or are you in the Army 24/7?' (Yes)

'Do you live in a tent on exercise all of the time or do you have other rooms inside in the warm, too?' (No, and yes)

'Is it true that you have to share rooms with men if you are a woman soldier?' (No)

'Do you get male soldiers chatting you up all the time?' (No)

'Do you get female soldiers chatting you up all the time?' (No)

As you can see, some kids really had let their imaginations run riot. At times, I could tell they had had these questions bubbling up in the back of their minds for months on end and could barely believe they were now allowed to ask them. Sometimes I wanted to laugh at their bizarre concerns, but of course I knew I never could – especially as I had been guilty of equally bad assumptions. Fake tan to Iraq, anyone? I tried to answer all of their questions as clearly as possible and to reassure them that there was room for all sorts in the Army.

It was so satisfying to explode the myths that they had created for themselves and I loved to see the look on their faces when I told them that I was only a few years older and had been to Iraq and still come back a girly girl, albeit one with a military commendation. They seemed to believe that anyone who had been to a warzone was an old grizzled man, staring into the distance and beginning every sentence with, 'Well, when I was at war...'

Some of those girls really reminded me of myself. I loved it when I would met them at one of the 'Look at Life' courses we ran and then spot them on the drill square a few months later, having joined up. The 'Look at Life' courses were for teenagers to come and stay on the barracks, experience going on exercise for two days and see what it was like on the assault course or the rifle range. They were certainly hectic work, but also some of the best fun I have ever had and I knew every minute of my time there was worth it as I was helping the kids to know what it was really like in the Armed Forces. I wanted every single one of them to follow their own ambitions instead of being held back by myths or stereotypes.

One lesson that I always loved doing with the girls was the one for 'Cam Cream'. That's the three-colour camouflage cream that soldiers wear on their faces and sometimes the back of their hands when on exercise. It's green, brown and black, the consistency of a creamy blusher or a child's face paints. The correct way to apply it is to wipe your fingers across the three colours and just smear your hand all the way across your face. This acts as a way of breaking up the texture of your face so that you are more effectively hidden in the bushes or undergrowth, or from a distance wherever you are. If you apply too little, patches of white face mark you out as obvious and if you put on too much, your teeth and the whites of your eyes immediately become obvious and you end up looking like Shrek! Another no-no is to apply a couple of faux-sophisticated little stripes on your cheekbones – a kind of fashion apache look which creates the image that you are off to a music festival, more than anything else.

Without fail, the girls would always become hysterical with giggles when confronted with the cam-cream lesson. There was always one who would carefully apply it as if it was make-up: green 'blusher' on the cheeks, brown 'lipstick' on the lips and a bit of black 'eye-shadow'. Madness! I would always have a laugh with them, doing my best to explain why this was not a good look.

Nevertheless, during that year I gained real insight into what motivates young women to want to serve, and what puts them off, as well as an overall view of what today's girls are like. We're not all *Nuts* magazine wannabe pin-ups or Paris Hilton-obsessed bimbos, like some newspapers would have us believe – there's a world of smart, ambitious and energetic women out there.

After my year in the recruiting team I was posted to Frimley Park in Surrey, which is a civilian and military hospital, where a lot of Army doctors and nurses work.

Military people are often treated there and I was taking on a clerical role. After travelling the country for so long it was nice to be in one place for a while, especially as it gave me a chance to see more of my friends. I had kept in touch with lots of my school friends, including Hayley.

For her birthday that year, she was given a voucher for a local photography studio, inviting her to have some professional shots taken, just for fun. As part of the package, she was allowed to take a friend and had invited me to go with her. I liked the idea of having some proper photographs to give to my mum and dad – I was always dashing around the country, half the time in Army gear, so the opportunity to have a decent professional photograph for their mantelpiece seemed too good to miss. After over four years spent in Army uniform with no make-up on, and six months in Iraq without a proper shower, I was well up for a day of glamour with an old friend. We really went the whole way, buying special outfits for the photos and making sure we did a great job with our hair and make-up. I still really like those images, even though I have had so many taken since.

Though I was pleased with the pictures, they didn't seem like anything special: to me, their value was sentimental. Hayley, however, thought otherwise and she came up with the idea that I should enter Miss England. At first, I didn't even think it was worth looking at the website – it seemed a ridiculous idea. For starters, there was the fact that I had never done any modelling or had anything at all to do with pageants during my teen years or childhood.

Then there was my assumption about pageant girls. It's probably the same as yours: scary pictures of girls with Vaseline on their teeth to get that extra sparkle, big lacquered hair that would explode into a fireball if it got too near a naked flame and terrifying square-cut talons instead of nails you can actually use. I hear you! But when I went online to do a bit of research, I realised that things have moved on a bit: there was no need for any slinky bikini photographs or even to type in your vital statistics: all you had to do was register and attach a shot of your face to enter a local heat. It didn't even have to be a professional photograph, a snapshot would do. The competition runs from September to July each year and it's now been going for over 60 years. My Miss England journey started in March 2008.

For me, it all began with Miss Tunbridge Wells, which is where my parents live. It was a simple online thing, where people would vote on a headshot of me. I sent off one of the photographs that I'd had done with Hayley and expected to get an email back after a day or two, saying something along the lines of 'thanks but no thanks'. I wasn't sure that I fitted the necessary criteria for a beauty queen at all, so I hadn't even put the fact that I was in the Army on the initial forms in case it held me back. But instead, I got an email back saying that they were excited to hear from me and asking me to fill in further forms. At this point I did admit what my profession was – after all, I was never going to feel ashamed of it.

The next stage of the process was getting people to vote from your local area and that voice from the BRIT School was still niggling away in the back of my mind, determined as ever to make sure I gave it my best shot. At first I did a few group emails, rallying the usual bunch of pals, and then I did some Facebook action, trying to scoop up a few more voters. But I reckoned I didn't have to stop at just people I knew, why not step things up a notch or two?

So I rang my local paper and said to them as casually as possible, 'Oh, is there any way you could put in a teeny little piece about me, to try and get people to text in?' I wasn't sure if phone calls like this ever worked, as I had never tried it before but I told myself that it couldn't do any harm and so I gave it a go. To my delight – and surprise – they said yes, and added that they wanted a picture, too.

I thought that might be the end of it – a weekend of local celebrity, a bit of something to gossip about next Friday night and a few more votes to see how far I could get. It all felt like a sprinkling of girly fun as the perfect antidote to the more blokey side to my job, but it went further than that: before I knew it, there was a reporter from the *Sun* at my doorstep.

CHAPTER FIVE

MEETING
THE PRESS

ONCE I was face to face with the journalist, I sensed that she wasn't pushy or sinister, but she really wanted my story. I knew that coverage like that might really help my chances in Miss Tunbridge Wells, or even Miss England, but I still wasn't convinced.

Lurking at the back of my mind was the thought that almost anyone could have turned up at my house, saying they were from the *Sun*. I didn't know what suspicious journalists were supposed to look like, but this woman seemed like someone you would walk past in Sainsbury's.

'I'd really like to do a piece on you,' she told me. 'You have a really interesting story.'

She seemed polite, smiley and honest, but I was still overwhelmed by her knocking on the front door of my childhood home.

The *Sun* being interested in me seemed extraordinary. It was one thing when I was Corporal Hodge, representing the Armed Forces, but this time they were interested in Kat: the whole story. Maybe they were testing me to see if I was a vain and gullible beauty queen.

I remembered how protective the Army press office had been with me the year before, and how glad I had been to have someone fielding my calls and making sure that I was talking to bona fide journalists. I didn't want to mess up, even though I was thrilled by the offer – I knew I couldn't say yes, just like that.

'Thank you so much for coming to find me,' I said. 'But I can't talk to you until I have spoken to my boss. I am not allowed to speak to the press without permission, especially if it's about work.'

She seemed to understand and left me with all of her details so that I could contact her again once I had spoken to the Army. I thanked her for her time, showed her to the door and then ran upstairs to my bedroom, slammed the door and let out a massive squeal of excitement. Immediately, the girls gathered round, wanting a blow-by-blow account of the conversation.

That weekend the piece ran in the local newspaper, which sent ripples of excitement among my friends. When I was out in town with the girls, people kept coming up to me all night, saying that they'd seen me in the paper. Tunbridge Wells is so small that everyone had seen it, which made me too scared to mention the *Sun* journalist.

Part of me was nervous that I wouldn't be given permission to do the interview while another part was still suspicious that the whole thing was a hoax. Nevertheless, there was a secret part of me thinking, just you wait and see what's coming next. It's going to be bigger than this...

Monday morning arrived faster than I ever want it to, and with it came time to scrape back my hair, put on my uniform and make an appointment to see my Commanding Officer. We rarely saw him, and not seeing him was probably for the best. If we passed him in the corridor, a polite smile was all that was needed: he was a 'speak when you're spoken to' kind of man.

Having said that, he always seemed like a good person. He was in his late forties or early fifties, with dark hair and a classically posh Army officer accent. Although tall, he was not a physically imposing man: he was quiet, an all-seeing observer rather than a red-faced shouting boss trying to make his presence felt by force. As a result, I always imagined that seeing him raise his voice would be utterly terrifying.

I often passed him in the corridor first thing in the morning, as he would regularly run the eight miles into work as part of his training. However, I had never been into his office before, though: you had to go through his secretary Julie if you wanted to see him. Usually, if you were in his office then you were in trouble.

I got into work extra-early and went to see Julie about fixing up an appointment in the next few days. She used to eat her lunch with us in our office, so I knew her quite well and was looking forward to getting her on side to arrange a meeting at the best possible time to catch the CO in a good mood. But she wasn't at her usual desk outside of the CO's office. Instead, he was there, sitting at his desk with the door ajar. I was prepared to speak to Julie, but I hadn't really psyched myself up to talk to the CO himself.

He looked away from his screen and peered over the top of his glasses. I stood to attention.

'Ah, Corporal Hodge – come on in.'

'Erm, good morning, sir. Is Julie not around?'

'No, no, no – she's off today. I'm on my own. What can I do to help?'

'Well, I was hoping to book an appointment to speak to you.'

'Great, I've got five minutes right now. Well, take a seat – talk to me.'

'Er, OK. Right now?'

I could hardly say no. When the CO invites you to sit down, it's not really an invitation, more like an order. I thought about shuffling off, muttering something about needing the toilet or it not being a good time right now, but instead I took a deep breath and decided to take the leap.

There were three risks I felt I was taking. Firstly, I didn't want the CO to think that I was being unprofessional, that I didn't care about my job or that I was bored by it. I was anxious that my ambition might seem as if my job was somehow 'not enough'. Secondly, my boss had only ever seen me in my Army combats, which are about as flattering as flannelette pyjamas, and with no make-up. There was nothing about me that could ever have suggested that I was going to enter a beauty pageant. He had never socialised with me so he didn't know what I looked like when I was in glam mode. Would he think I was deranged for entering the competition? And finally, I knew that everyone's stereotype of Miss England was 'girls in bikinis'. I was effectively starting a conversation that would be inviting my boss to imagine me in a bikini. Eeeeew!

But this was not the time to let my anxieties get the better of me. After all, I had spent hours on the Sunday preparing a little folder of cuttings about the competition, printing off sections of the website and putting together my argument: I wanted it to be airtight, for minimum humiliation. As ever, preparation was key. There is a strong charity element to Miss England and I would be able to represent and possibly change the image of women in the Armed Forces. Those were my reasons for doing the competition and my strongest arguments with my CO. It was up to me to overturn any preconceived notions he might have about the competition. This was my responsibility and if I lost my nerve the chance might be gone forever. Time to bite the bullet… I pressed my nails into the palms of my hands and began.

The CO gestured to a big black leather chair opposite his desk. Then he glanced at his computer and told me: 'I won't be two minutes – I just need to finish something up here.'

He tapped away at the keyboard while I looked around his office, at the photographs and plaques on the walls and his pace stick mounted on his desk. The noise and bustle of the rest of the regiment seemed miles away on the other side of his door. Inside, I could almost hear my heart thundering away in my chest.

Then he looked up from the screen, peered over his glasses and said: 'So, what can I help you with?'

I stuttered and spluttered my way through the explanation of why I had entered Miss Tunbridge Wells and why the *Sun* wanted to interview me, all the while trying to sit in the most upright, professional manner that I could.

Naturally, he was obliged to ask me lots of questions but the tone he was asking them in strongly suggested that he had already made up his mind about the situation. But I had started this conversation, and I wasn't going to back out of it now.

'Riii-iight. So what do you hope to achieve from this?' he asked with a slight frown.

'Well, Miss England isn't just a training camp for lads' mag girls, it's an institution that really values women with a bit of spirit. There are sections for skills and achievements, not just glamour.'

'Mmmm...'

'There is a massive amount of charity work involved and I would definitely be supporting Help for Heroes as my charity. I think I could raise a lot of money and awareness.'

'Ye-ees.'

'I intend to support and promote the Army throughout. I want to transform the image of women in the Forces and show that girls like me can be good soldiers, too.'

'I see... There is still a lot of prancing about in bikinis, isn't there? How does that square with your job?'

'These days, you don't even have to wear a bikini if you don't want to – you can choose a one-piece. I would do that. And you won't get anywhere in the competition without proper talent and hard work.'

I assumed that he was also being mindful not to come across as some kind of 1970s sex pest boss, reacting with a delighted, 'Oh ho *hooo*, I'm sure you look delightful in a bikini!' That would have been a total cringe, and I was relieved that he was at least giving me the chance to say my bit. When I stopped talking, I listened to the pounding from my chest: I had given it my best shot and I felt that I had made a good case.

'It seems like a great idea, but it's not just my decision to make,' he finally told me. 'I will have to pass it up a little higher, just in case.'

'Oh thank you, sir!' I grinned – and got out of his office as fast as I could.

I couldn't believe it: I left his office half-smiling, half-frowning. Persuading my CO had been much easier than I had anticipated, but there was still the question of what my colleagues would think. I couldn't get the thought out of my head. Am I about to be judged for this? Will my team think that being in the Army is just not enough for me or that I really overrate myself for wanting to give this a shot? I wanted to prove that I was more than the Army stereotype – that we *all* were – but I didn't want to lose friends over it either.

A few hours later I was sitting at my desk, chatting to the girls in the office, chuckling about my chances in Miss England. Kayleigh, the girl who sat next to me, had already logged on to the website and was trawling through the prize list, eyeing up the goods.

'Oooh, look! Could I come with you on that holiday?' she was shrieking. At that moment the CO walked in. Silence.

'Corporal Hodge, could you pop into my office, please?' he asked, looking round at the rest of the team. They all stared at each other, then quickly shifted their gaze to their computer screens, pulling up pages of official work.

'Yes, sir.' I followed him in and stayed standing to attention, cheeks burning with embarrassment at having been caught messing around at my desk.

'You don't have to stand like that, you can sit down.'

'OK, thank you.'

'I've got the permission from the Army press office. There shouldn't be a problem in you doing the interview. If you want to be in any other newspapers, just let me know as we want to know what's coming out before the rest of the world does. I trust you will continue to take your responsibilities to the Army seriously, though.'

'Yes, sir! Absolutely. And thank you very much.'

I walked back to my desk as fast as my now-wobbly legs would carry me. As soon as there was a quiet moment in the office, I called the reporter from the *Sun* and arranged the interview.

That weekend, I went back home to Tunbridge Wells and the reporter and a photographer came out to see me. Having explained myself under such scrutiny to my CO, I felt confident talking to the reporter; it was the photographs that I was now nervous about for they marked my début in the national press as Kat, rather than Corporal Hodge. I hoped that all that time in stage school would help me out again!

The girls and I chatted about it for ages and I decided to wear red: I wanted to choose a strong look and stick to it, and I have always felt safe in red. There was no point in putting in the effort and getting the permission to do the interview, then fluffing it by being too timid to look my absolute best.

I've done so many photo shoots since, but this one will stay in my memory forever. The photographer wanted to take the pictures outside, so we went down to my local park. Despite the great care I had taken over my look, the one thing I hadn't prepared for was the weather – it was absolutely freezing! It was February and there I was, standing around in a cocktail dress in a park, with my heels sinking slowly into the mud for about an hour and half! My hair was blowing around everywhere, whipping into my eyes and sticking to my lip-gloss. The wind was giving me a rather more ruddy glow that I had intended when I'd applied my blusher hours before and it was hard to keep a sincere smile for more than a few seconds as I was shivering and my teeth were chattering.

I can so clearly remember standing in the cold in that dress, but what I remember even more is the moment when I opened the paper to see that they had only used a headshot: I could have been wearing my coat, even my dressing gown! I could have been wearing anything.

My consolation was that it was a lovely piece. It's impossible to ever know what the press is going to say about you, but once I had got over my shock at them using a headshot and decided the piece was fair, I pretty much forgot about the whole thing. I thought it had just been a bit of fun, and that that would be that: it was back to work, to prove to the regiment that I was still a committed soldier.

It seems the extra publicity helped though, as a few weeks later I was back at my desk when I felt my mobile phone buzzing in my pocket. When I looked at the screen, I saw that it was the Miss England office calling me. I didn't want to be seen taking the call during office hours, so I quickly looked round the room and spotted an opportunity: the broom cupboard. I leapt into it, and shuffled things around so there was a bit of space for me to stand up, guided by the glowing green light of my mobile's screen.

'Um, hello?' I answered, trying to sound as glamorous as anyone ever has from inside a broom cupboard.

'Hello, my name is Angie Beasley – I'm the director of Miss England. Is that Kat Hodge?'

'Yes. Yes, it is.' (I could feel a mop brushing against the back of my hair).

'It's lovely to speak to you. I'm happy to let you know that you are going to be crowned Miss Tunbridge Wells and will go through to the semi-finals of Miss England on June 14th. You will be one of 60 going through.'

'Oh wow, thank you so much for letting me know!' (I was grinning at a shelf of Toilet Duck, unable to keep my glee to myself).

'We've been getting a lot of calls about you since you were in the *Sun*. I've got lots of press interested in talking to you, and I just want to let you know that I think it is fantastic that you are in the Armed Forces. We all do at Miss England.'

(Now I wanted to hug the mop and kiss the Toilet Duck).

'That's great news! I nearly left my job off the entrance form – I thought it would count me out.'

'No, if anything it seems the opposite is true. I will email you details soon, but it's been great to talk to you.'

'Thank you so much, and you... Thank you for calling. Thank you.'

(OK Kat, you can shut up now, I sensed the broom thinking to itself).

I was through to the semi-finals! The glamour began to

kick in almost as soon as the adrenaline now. A week later, I was asked if I could take a day off work as I had been given the opportunity to take part in some promotional activity for the competition. It was a shoot to celebrate the launch of the Miss England bikini: a red-and-white bikini with a sequined St George cross pattern, which was to be part of the official merchandise. However, the idea of making my entrance onto the pageant scene in a bikini – and a white one at that – was not one that filled me with excitement: the chance to meet some of the team and to hang out with a few of the other girls in a non-competitive way was too much to resist, though. Nothing ventured, nothing gained, so I took a deep breath and said yes to the invitation. It meant a trip up to London, where I'd meet some of the other competitors for the first time, as well as the then Miss England, Georgia Horsley.

It was no problem to take the day off and a couple of weeks later, in April 2008, I headed up to London on a sunny Friday morning. The shoot was to involve eight of us in the Miss England bikinis, on that famous London zebra crossing in tribute to the Beatles' *Abbey Road* album cover.

Yes. A bikini. In public... Terrifying! It wasn't just that I didn't want to look lardy in public in a bikini, but once you're in a bikini, people have almost no other way of judging you. Unless you are actually heading for the beach, the fact that you're wearing one instantly puts the suggestion out there that you have nothing more to offer.

If you go to your local high street and stop fifty people, I bet they would all come up with one of the following ten clichés about pageant girls. It's the same the world over: everyone thinks it's all about these things, and these things alone:

Big, blonde, plastic hair
Big, brown, plastic boobs
Vaseline slicked onto teeth
Enormous high heels, possibly transparent
Highly flammable, satiny dresses
Sparkles and sequins
Fingernails that could take your eye out
Terrifying pushy mothers
Vague waffling about 'world peace'
...And really, *really* stupid girls.

As the train zoomed towards London my stomach filled with dread at the prospect of meeting some of those monster girls. What if they were all walking clichés? Would I fit in? Would it be worth me trying to pursue the rest of the competition if it meant being surrounded by girls like that? At this point I had never done any modelling or had anything to do with the beauty pageant world, so I had no idea what the reality would present.

There was one other small problem: my fake tan. In a moment of over-enthusiasm (or panic, more likely) the night before the shoot, I had rushed to the nearest tanning salon, which had a spare appointment. I had begged for the darkest colour they had, as quickly as possible. All I was thinking was: white bikini, need tan. Big mistake. Huge.

When I woke up 12 hours later, I gasped: I wasn't sun-kissed, I was mahogany! I had been given the full creosote treatment and so had my bed sheets. Grim! I ran to the shower and tried to scrub off as much as possible, but all I was left with were bizarre tidemarks all over my body. What would the professional pageant princesses say when they saw my tan of shame? I need not have worried.

As I walked into the sports club where we were changing for the shoot, I immediately realised that this was a friendly environment. The air was far from being thick with bitchiness; the vibe was more like a girly sleepover. There were bags all over the floor and brushes, make-up and accessories on every available counter. I was shocked. There were girls smiling at me and offering to help with my make-up. And they weren't airheads, they were normal: there was a trainee barrister, a doctor and gaggle of bright students.

There was one girl who definitely stood out, though: Georgia Horsley, who was Miss England that year. I just remember looking at her and thinking, 'Oh my *God*, you're *gorgeous*! What am I doing here? What have I got myself involved in? I'm never going to be her...'

But again my preconceptions were proved wrong when she turned out to be another lovely girl. She's really organised and had got herself ready in plenty of time to help everyone else out.

I did my make-up and put on the bikini, a gorgeous fluffy white dressing gown and the new silver shoes I had been told I needed for the shoot. Moments later, we were lined up by the door in height and hair colour order. I was behind Georgia, who is blonde. Once we were in position, someone walked by with their arms out and a voice cried: 'Dressing gowns off, girls!'

I followed the line-up out of the door onto the street and was immediately hit by the blinding flashes of a huge barrage of cameramen. All of the traffic on the street had been stopped and the police were surrounding the area to make sure we were safe. A huge crowd of passing shoppers had gathered to see what all the hubbub was about. So many pairs of eyes looking at us...

I was shaking with nerves. Literally. I was shaking so much that I stumbled in my new shoes and tripped, stepping out of the left one. Luckily the girl behind me saw and stopped to help me – a nasty domino situation was narrowly avoided. What wasn't avoided was me having to lean over to rearrange my shoe in front of the rows of press. I was feeling self-conscious enough, standing next to Miss England in a bikini, but then as I bent down to replace the shoe on my foot I felt my stomach squish up and was aware that I was giving the press a major boob shot.

Luckily it was only a moment, though and before long I was doing my best to pose confidently with the rest of the team. But I had no experience, so I had no idea of what I was really meant to be doing. A fortnight earlier I had imagined myself there, thinking, this is the dream! In fact, as I stood there, trying to get myself in a flattering position for each of the cameramen gathered round, I found myself wondering: what the hell am I doing here?

All I could hear was a scrum of men shouting at us, so I never knew which camera to look at when, or how to get a good pose at any time. I could have studied as much of *America's Next Top Model* as I wanted beforehand, but even I know my best poses wouldn't have worked in front of so many cameras. Flustered, I kept shifting and shuffling around – this wasn't the fun day of glamour that I had had in mind. After about half an hour, I had a moment of clarity: you might never get the chance to do something like this again. You can't do anything about what you look like now, so just enjoy it. Smile. Smile like you mean it!

It was a good job that I decided to relax, as the photo shoot that I had thought would last for about ten minutes eventually went on for an hour and a half. We were arranged into various groups and sub groups, but were out there for much longer than I had ever imagined we would be. By the end of it I was having such a laugh with the other girls that I had pretty much forgotten I was in a bikini.

Once the formalities were over we changed into summery frocks and were treated to champagne and cupcakes in the sports club where we had changed. I felt like the winner of a reality show challenge, being lavished with such a day of glamour and luxury, especially when we were whisked off to the launch party at Café de Paris in Leicester Square. It was a far cry from the Sergeants' Mess.

We all got stuck into the bubbly and the dancing. I loved having the chance to banter with all the girls once we were out of our bikinis and no longer had the cameras in our faces. After a few hours I glanced around the room and took a moment to absorb the atmosphere. We were there with a choice selection of D-listers like Gary Lucy and some ex-*Big Brother* housemates. I noticed that some of the girls were getting down to some serious drinking – and flirting. And I spotted that one of the ex-*Big Brother* guys had turned up in Army uniform. This struck me as bizarre, and slightly disrespectful – our uniform is worn for a reason, not a fashion statement.

As I sat and drank in the vibe it struck me that while I like the perks and the glamour, the life of a minor celebrity wasn't exactly for me. Some of the girls were now pretty drunk – either that or seriously star-struck. This seemed like a good opportunity to start the process of noticing who was only interested in drinking champagne with micro-celebs and who actually understood the words 'role model'. But I decided to live for the moment and danced the night away, mindful not to get caught up in the undertow of the piss-heads. And I was on the last train home, careful to have enjoyed only a couple of glasses – I knew I had to be up bright and early for my first portfolio pictures. I barely had time to cleanse, tone and moisturise before collapsing into bed. If the Army had taught me anything, it was to grab sleep whenever you can.

Part of the prize for winning Miss Tunbridge Wells was to have my first solo photo shoot of images for my portfolio. I had been told to turn up with a bare face and clean, but unstyled, hair. As if facing the camera solo wasn't daunting enough, I was dreading what a selection of professionals would think of me with no make-up on. 'Another blooming delusional' was what I suspected.

It was 8am when I arrived at Fresh Studios for the shoot and there was no Hayley to keep me company this time. In a way I wish she had been there, as it was the day that I realised the potential pitfalls of being photographed. I was not feeling at my most beautiful, especially when I saw the stunning photographs lining the walls. The first one that I recognised was Georgia Horsley herself, and there were several other celebrities beaming down as I walked through to Make-up from Reception.

I just hope they can work some magic to make me look like that, I thought.

My eyes lit up when I saw the hair and make-up room, though – it was a girly paradise! There were rows and rows of colours, bottles, brushes and bits. The huge mirrors were lined with glowing bulbs, the room was buzzing with people discussing looks and ideas.

I had a suitcase of outfits with me, which the stylists immediately started to sift through, deciding which look would go with which photographic backdrop. Everyone

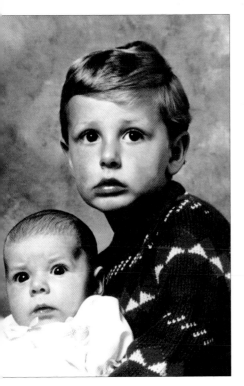
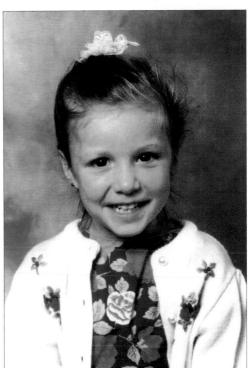

e as a little girl – with my brother Byran (*above left* and *below*) and showing off my
eeky grin aged three.

Above: In Sea Cadets, aged 13.

Below: With my friend Leonie, aged 16.

above left: Doing my Basic Training in 2004.

above right: With my friend Stacey in Iraq – bringing a touch of glamour to the camp!

below: On patrol in Iraq in 2005 – the kids there were so lovely.

Above: With the medal I received when I came back from Iraq.

Below: As Miss Tunbridge Wells 2008, getting ready for the bikini launch.

bove left: Miss England at last! © *Graham Stone*

bove right: A shot from one of my modelling sessions. Being Miss England
)ened up a whole new world of photoshoots and public appearances. © *Fresh Academy*

elow: Another Miss England promotional photo. © *Steve Dock*

Above: Backstage at Miss Every Model.

Below: Attempting to play golf at Miss World!

bove: With Laura (Miss Ireland) on a rainy safari – we were so glad we hadn't glammed
 like the other Miss World contestants!

elow: Me and Laura with Miss Wales, Lucy.

Above: 'Team GB' at the Miss World finals – Miss Scotland, Miss Wales, me, Miss Ireland and Miss Northern Ireland.

Below: With some of the other Miss World girls – I'm 5'9" so you can imagine how tall they all were!

was chatty and reassuring, there was no question that they thought I didn't fit in. I loved the girly atmosphere as well – everyone there but the photographer was a woman not too much older than me. They all seemed as excited as I was about getting me to look great for the pictures and there was no sleazy old man trying to persuade me to undo that extra button.

After an hour in the make-up chair, I opened my eyes and was stunned by what I saw: I had no idea that I could look such a glamour queen! It really was amazing make-up – super-deluxe, but not tacky. If I'd been able to describe it back then, I would have asked for exactly that look. I couldn't wait to get in front of the camera.

The photographer had me try several different backgrounds and outfits while a team of stylists helped me pose to my best advantage. They had music blaring and it was a fun, collaborative atmosphere. I felt like a real princess.

'Lift your head now.' Snap!

'Smile over there.' Flash!

'Turn your left leg in a little.' Click!

After some properly glamorous shots the team asked if I'd like to do some images in my Army combats. I knew that I wasn't allowed to wear them with styled hair and make-up, but then again these were just shots for my own portfolio, not the media. The photographer suggested I wore my combat trousers with the Miss England bikini top to make a nice contrast and to show the two sides to my personality – the beauty queen and the soldier. I did think it would make a nice shot, but I explained that I wasn't allowed to be photographed in uniform with styling.

'Don't worry about it,' he reassured me. 'It's a once-in-a-lifetime chance to get pics of you looking your best and they're not for the media. Remember, they're just for your own portfolio and you alone.'

So I agreed to do some shots in the bikini top with a military shirt open above it. The make-up artist came and put some green stripes across my cheeks, but I tried to smudge them as quickly as possible. I didn't want to look as if I was taking the mick. Again, I was reassured that they were personal pictures so I could relax and do whatever I wanted. It was a treat, a prize, they kept telling me. I didn't want to get a reputation for being difficult on shoots, so I went along with the fun of the day. Everyone was really interested in my job and I was flattered by that.

When I went into the edit room to see the images that had been taken I felt a rush of pride at how great I looked: I certainly didn't look like the same girl who had nervously arrived a few hours before. I was thrilled and ended up picking a big selection of shots for my portfolio. After all, I didn't know if I would ever have the opportunity to be photographed professionally again.

There was absolutely nothing sleazy about the situation on the day and they were a really professional team, but I was much more naïve then; I didn't know how much things can be misinterpreted. There's always one shot that looks a little different out of context – and of course that's the one that came to bite me on the bum.

Exhilarated after my 48 hours of London glamour, I headed back to barracks that night and went to bed early. I woke up buzzing, as did my phone. When I looked at it on the bedside table, I saw that I had dozens of missed calls and texts. Most of them were saying more or less the same thing: You're in the *News of the World*!

I was excited, thinking they might have used some of the images taken on Friday's bikini shoot. Perhaps my face and maybe one of my mahogany legs would be in shot next to Georgia? I hopped in the car and went to pick up a paper. As I stopped at traffic lights, I saw my phone buzz again on the driver's seat. It was a text from Stacey: 'Oh man, are you in trouble or what..!'

Eh? What could that mean? Why would I be in trouble? The worst thing that I could think of was that someone I had known when I was a kid had seen me in the *Sun* and done a fake kiss-and-tell on me. I just don't have that many skeletons to hide!

But it all became clear when I got to the shop and flicked open the *News of the World*. There I was, pages four and five: nearly two pages of Kat. In her bikini. And her combats! My jaw dropped. I grabbed a few copies and fumbled in my wallet for the change to pay for them.

'Is that you?' asked the guy behind the till.

Instead of being excited and proud about having my image in the paper, I just tried to avoid his gaze and mumbled 'Yeah, kind of' before getting out of there as fast as I could.

The 'private' photographs that I had had taken only 24 hours before were now a major feature in the *News of the World*. They didn't use any interview or quotes from me, just the headlines COMBATS TO CATWALK and SQUADDIE GOING FOR MISS ENGLAND. There was a massive link to the photographer's website, where you could find the rest of the images of me. In my Army combats and bikini top. With a lot of make-up. This spelt big trouble.

How had I allowed this to happen? In the past, I had been so fastidious about getting the right permissions for interviews. I had wanted to make the Army proud of me, not disappointed. Would my boss think I was a slapper or just an idiot? Neither was great. The rest of that day was spent calling people for advice and in between chats, taking small breaks to sit on the edge of my bed and panic. I felt totally betrayed by the studio. It was the slowest Sunday of all time.

That Monday morning, I slowly opened one eye and then the other. Damn, I wasn't ill! I would have to turn up at work. It's amazing how much can change in a day. There was another crop of texts and calls on my phone when I turned it on, but this time my stomach lurched when I went to look at them. Butterflies of excitement seemed like a distant dream.

I drove to work as slowly as possible and walked to the

office, with my head down, hoping no one would notice me. Every step felt as if I was walking a thousand miles in lead boots. The Army had done nothing but support and encourage me and now I was being featured in a raunchy pose in one of the country's biggest-selling tabloids. I was expecting remorseless teasing at best. At worst, my reputation indelibly tainted with a lads' mag image. Would I even have a job to go to, come Tuesday?

It felt as if I was trying to reconcile the two sides of my personality, while offending no one: I wanted to prove that I could be more than a stereotypical soldier and more than a cookie-cutter pageant girl, but suddenly I was at risk of seeming like less than either. I knew I could still be a good soldier but would my seniors believe me? Meanwhile, I didn't want to say anything to jeopardise my chances at Miss England after I had been given such a great opportunity to model for them.

I sat at my desk. No one else was in yet. I started working. No one came in for a while. Maybe I had got away with it? If things were just quiet today, there would be new newspapers and soon the *News of the World* would be forgotten. Every time the door opened, I looked up with a start, wondering when my inevitable confrontation would take place. It wasn't too long.

'Corporal Hodge, would you mind stepping into my office for a moment?'

My line manager was standing at my desk. In her mid-forties, well respected and not unusually brutal, she was the last person I wanted to let down. But she was a play-by-the-rules kind of boss, so deep down I had known she would get to me eventually. I followed her into her office and remained standing as she went to her desk. As I got on with her, usually I would just sit down but I knew it was best not to do so on this occasion.

'Go on then, sit down,' she instructed me, as she sat at her own desk. I perched on the chair facing her. The *News of the World* was on her desk.

'So,' she said with a flourish, as she flipped the pages open. There I was. I could see now more clearly than ever that the way I was wearing my Army shirt open over the bikini looked as if I was mid-way through a provocative strip.

I blushed.

'What do you have to say about this?'

I took a deep breath and started talking. My heart was in my throat. Everything that had been in my head for the past 24 hours came burbling out.

'I'm so sorry, ma'am. I didn't mean for this to happen, ma'am. I was told that they were going to be personal photographs, ma'am. I know I was never supposed to pose in my combats with hair and make-up, ma'am.'

I kept calling her 'Ma'am', hoping that she would somehow know how much I respected her and the Armed Forces; also my job. I tried to explain my mistake, but the more I talked, the more I felt as if I was making myself sound like an idiot.

'Well, the Commanding Officer spoke to me about it this

morning and he certainly isn't happy. This is not something that you had permission to do and it certainly is not something that you would have received permission to do. I am going to have to have a chat with him now that I have spoken to you and I am sure that he will want to have a word with you, too.

'You have made a mockery of your uniform. To your credit, you do seem to realise this.'

I thought back to when I'd spotted the *Big Brother* housemate in his Army uniform and how insulted I had felt to see him wearing it as a fashion statement. If only she could understand the irony of how well I understood what it felt like to see your uniform mocked. Somehow I sensed that filling her in with the details of my D-list night out at Café de Paris was not going to help her take my apologies seriously, though.

Shortly after that, I was called in to see the CO. This time, he wasn't the same polite, mild-mannered boss who had given me permission to be photographed in the *Sun*. Instead, he gave me a stern talking to and I was shaking by the time I left his office.

I am not one for crying but when I closed his office door behind me, I had to walk to the toilets as fast as I possibly could. Within seconds, I had slammed the door behind me and burst into noisy sobs. I cried my heart out, devastated that I had brought the Army into disrepute and terrified that I was now facing the sack. Afterwards, I called my friends in tears and tried to listen to their reassurances that things were not over for me yet, but I wasn't so sure.

I returned to my desk in silence and slid onto my chair. For the next three days, I just kept my head down and got on with the job as best I could. I took the merciless teasing from my colleagues at meal times and breaks, and did my best not to be seen laughing about it in front of any seniors. All the while, my mobile continued to go crazy with offers from magazines such as *Zoo* and *Nuts*. I said no thanks to everything and explained the situation to Angie from the Miss England office. She was very understanding and made sure that those pictures were never used again.

Meanwhile, I did my utmost to avoid contact with my boss until I knew what the situation was. I knew I was being watched. If I had a piece of paper that needed to be signed, I would wait until she had gone to the bathroom or for a cup of tea, then put it in her in tray when she wasn't there. For a few days, I tried to become the invisible employee instead of the attention seeker. Towards the end of the week, I faced the final verdict.

'Corporal Hodge, could I see you in my office, please?'

My stomach lurched.

'Sit down, then.'

I did as I was told.

'I have received an email from the Colonel of the Corps. He asked me to congratulate you for promoting the Adjutant General's Corps in the national press. You were wearing your stable belt in those photographs and we have actually had some positive feedback from that coverage.'

Oh. My. God. I hadn't even realised it at the time but I had been wearing my stable belt, the elasticated belt branded in the colours of our corps. But instead of getting me into further trouble, it had actually saved me. I was identified as a real soldier, not a wannabe. Seeing the red-blue-red stripes of the Adjutant General's Corps in such a big paper certainly helped everyone realise what a great chance I had been given for promoting the Army.

'We trust that the nature of your pose was just a one-off. If you can give us your assurance that that is the case, we will understand that this was a situation born of your relative naïvety, not any desire to provoke or rebel.'

'Yes, ma'am, of course! Never again, absolutely.'

'No more bikinis. No more make-up. No more big hair.'

'No, never, ma'am.'

'And if you ever plan to be featured in the media again, you will continue to need our permission.'

'Yes, of course, ma'am.'

'It has, however, been noted that the online comments have all been very positive about you representing the best of Britain and all that the Armed Forces can be.'

'Thank you, ma'am. I do understand my mistake, I can assure you.'

'That will be all.'

'Thank you, ma'am.'

The office door closed softly behind me and I felt an

enormous weight lift from my shoulders. I had learned a difficult lesson the hard way. From that day on, I knew that I'd never pose in my Army uniform again. I cannot trust anyone outside the Forces to respect it in the way that my seniors do: it's not a costume. There isn't always someone to look out for you when you're in front of a camera, so you can't do anything that you wouldn't want to be seen doing in the press. I am my own responsibility and now I take that seriously.

CHAPTER SIX

THE SEMI-FINALS

M Y PRECARIOUS first experience of trying to combine work and Miss England had shaken me up a little but had ultimately given me the confidence that, with a bit of concentration, I could juggle the two roles. Sadly, I couldn't magic up a few extra hours in the day, though: preparing for Miss England while holding down such an active full-time job meant I never stopped. Unlike the majority of other contestants, who were mostly students or models, I could not fit my schedule around what needed to be done for the competition so I was rushing home from work to practise my skills, work on my outfits, put together my talent video and to make sure that I had every administrative detail seen to.

I had from April until June 2008 to get everything ready for the semi-finals. My working hours were

8am–5pm and I was being asked to do a lot of press and radio interviews. During those three months, I don't think I had an hour to myself: I wanted to say yes to every opportunity I had to promote my bid for Miss England, but it left me with no time for anything else. Even on the weekends, news crews asked if they could follow me around. It was complete madness.

One of the biggest tasks I had to sort out was making a 'talent' video for the semi-finals. I decided that if I were going to be true to myself, I'd have to do something a little bit different from the usual singing or dancing, which so often seemed to dominate the section. After all, my time at the BRIT School had already taught me that I was never going to be the next Mariah Carey, so my strength would always have to lie in being different from the other girls, not trying to be the best at being the same.

By this stage I had a regular contact at the Army press office because of the number of interviews I was being asked to do. His name is Simon Taylor and he used to be in the Army himself, but now works for the press team. During those first few months he acted as a barrier for me, protecting me from shady journalists of the kind that I was worried that the *Sun* journalist might have been. Simon made sure that I only did interviews I was comfortable with and were within the right code of conduct for my day job in the Army. He helped me make decisions so I wouldn't end up with shifty reporters pulling a fast one on me.

COMBAT TO CATWALK

What I loved most about the press I was doing wasn't actually the attention, but the fact that I had a buddy with me throughout: Chloe Marshall. Chloe was another Miss England contestant who was getting a lot of attention that year. In her case, it was because she is an absolutely stunning girl. And she is also a size 16. It was a year of real change for Miss England, with the two of us on our separate missions to overthrow the existing stereotypes about beauty and role models. In years gone by, it had just been blonde robo-babes and the winner who had received any attention at all. This year, things were different: we were two chatty, confident girls, travelling the country together with something real to talk about and having a right laugh on the way.

Chloe only lived 10 minutes away from my Army camp in Surrey so we'd often get the train up to London together. We'd meet at the station, our hair in heated rollers, and spend the entire journey chatting and doing our pageant make-up. I soon discovered that it doesn't matter how many frowns uptight commuters give you for having your hair still in rollers as long as you have someone with you to giggle about it. People on the train would regularly look at us as if we were maniacs, but I just didn't care. And nor did Chloe – we had bigger things on our mind than what they thought.

During that time we were featured in *Hello*, *OK!*, *Closer*, *Pick Me Up* and even got to feature in a Euro 2008 video with Sven-Göran Eriksson. It was our first experience of being interviewed by a lot of different journalists on the same topic and before long, both of us realised we had a kind of script that we'd be sticking to. After a while, they all seem to ask the same question, over and again.

It never ceased to surprise me that journalists would regularly forget or ignore the fact that I had quite a demanding job – even though that was the very thing that was interesting them about me! I was constantly getting calls at my desk at work, having to check my mobile during tea breaks and trying not to let it interfere with my main job.

Within weeks, that broom cupboard where I had first spoken to Angie from was becoming something of a safe haven. Sometimes radio producers would call for a telephone interview without checking where I was, and would be on air already so I'd suddenly have to duck into the cupboard for a bit of peace and quiet. On other occasions, I would have time to request proper permission and find a quiet room in which to do the interview, but on more than one occasion it was suddenly announced to me that I was on air and I would find myself diving back in with the mops.

I was amazed by how few boundaries the press has and quite quickly learnt to be cautious. Chloe didn't have a day job, so if she was contacted then she could give whoever it was her full attention, but often it would be my mum who was left bearing the brunt of things for me. Journalists would randomly turn up unannounced at my childhood home and say nonchalantly: 'Oh, hi there! We thought we'd just pop round and see how Kat was getting along.'

When Mum sensibly tried to question them about who they were and why they were there, they would usually end up admitting that they weren't friends she hadn't met, but members of the press.

'Well, we thought we'd swing by and have a quick chat with her about how things are going with Miss England,' they'd say, as if it was entirely normal.

She would then remind them that I didn't actually live there full time, but was stationed on the Army camp. And then they'd have to find me via the Army press office, like everyone else. I always found that kind of approach very invasive and it made me apprehensive about what the downside of success in the public eye could really be. What would happen if they were interested in me for all the wrong reasons?

There was no way that I was going to let those negative aspects stop me in the competition, though: I figured it was about the way I handled it, and how I could surprise and inspire people with a different image. I wanted as many of them as possible to know about my attempt to become Miss England. By this stage, I was getting national exposure – more than some *X Factor* or *Big Brother* contestants do. It was my theory that the more people found out, the less of an option there would be for me to lose my nerve and back out. It was just the same as when

I decided to join the Army and made sure that I told absolutely anyone who would listen; a kind of safety net to ensure any last-minute nerves would never let me get away with a discreet shuffle away from my dreams.

While we were waiting to do a radio interview one day I mentioned to Simon Taylor that I wanted to put together a film demonstrating my key military skills for the talent section of Miss England, but would I need the Army's permission? And how could I shoot it? Simon loved the idea and went to town sorting it out for me, setting up the whole shoot with Army cameramen.

I wanted to show off all the skills I had learned from being in the Army, so we went to the assault course at the Royal Military Academy Sandhurst to film it in May 2008. Sandhurst is the training college for all Army officers and has the biggest assault course, set among the most scenic grounds. I spent a whole day there, doing the course again and again for the cameras: climbing the rope wall, running through tyres, scrambling through netting with a face full of mud, and of course doing a few classic push-ups. That day I did more training than I have ever done in my life, just repeating it all again and again until the crew had caught the right camera angles. Next up, we spent a couple of hours with me doing classic drill moves with my rifle on the square. I was shaking with tiredness, but then it was time to head for the rifle range.

When we arrived at the ranges there were some regular trainees practising, who were more than a little confused when I turned up with a film crew in tow. After about fifteen minutes one of them walked past and looked right at me before nodding to himself.

'Oh, it's that Combat Barbie,' he said to himself, as he wandered off.

Yes, it certainly was! And I was thrilled with how good the finished DVD looked – it was worth all the hours of running around as the angles seemed properly professional and true to how I wished to be perceived. All sides of my military persona were represented: I wanted Miss England to find out just how tough a beauty queen could really be.

It was a good job that I got that day of intense training in when we were making the DVD, as I had no time for extra exercise during the rest of the run-up to the semi-finals. Obviously I trained every day with the Army – runs, circuit training or some kind of outdoor exercise – but I didn't have a spare moment to do anything more focused on toning or definition. In the end I found myself hoping that the nervous energy and the fact that I was running around in a bit of a frenzy all day would be enough to see me through.

The semi-finals were held on 14 June at Champney's Springs Health Farm in the countryside outside the city of Leicester. When I drove up the path to the hotel itself, it was such a beautiful moment: the place looked like something out of a film and I could scarcely believe I was there. I felt a shiver of excitement that I was going to be staying somewhere like that for two days. It was a far cry from my Army experiences in Iraq!

When I got up to my room, I unfurled my evening gown and glanced at it nervously. Shouldn't that be 'excitedly'? Well, yes, I suppose it should have been, but I was nervous because I had never tried it on before. I'd been so busy with my other preparations – the press, the DVD, my actual job – that I'd forgotten to sort myself out with an evening dress until the very last minute! In the end, one of the officers at work had saved my bacon. It turned out that his sister had a bridal-wear shop in Tunbridge Wells and she offered to loan me a dress. It was stunning, even though it was really meant to be a wedding dress. You couldn't tell though, as it was pink and covered in Swarovski crystals. It had only been delivered to work the day before, so I had packed a very average black gown that I knew fitted me, grabbed the pink bridal dress and hoped for the best. I must admit my heart was hammering when I reached behind to try and do the zip up the back. Luck was on my side: it was a perfect fit.

Once I had confronted that little drama, I changed out of the summery blue frock I had arrived in and put on what was required for the first round – some smart sportswear. I put on cute Pineapple tracksuit bottoms and a vest top, but when I got downstairs to the reception room, I was a bit taken aback to see just how many of the 50 girls in my semi-final were wearing tiny hot pants as 'sportswear'.

While we were all sitting around in there, Angie from Miss England came up to me with a half-anxious, half-excited look on her face.

'Oh, um, hello Kat,' she said with a smile.

'Hi, how can I help?' I replied, trying to sound as bright and breezy and professional as I possibly could. I knew what a key figure Angie was.

'Could I have a quick word with you out here?' she asked.

'Of course.' I followed her out into the corridor. Her already-soft voice was almost entirely absorbed by the plush carpets in the hotel, she was speaking so discreetly: it seemed she really didn't want any of the other girls to know what was going on.

'Well, we've got some gentlemen from Channel 5 News here and they'd like to follow you around for the next couple of days, to do a bit of a diary of how you are getting along, what Combat Barbie's chances of reaching the final are, that kind of thing. Are you OK with that?'

I felt so divided and excited at the same time. On the one hand it was incredibly exciting that they were interested in me. But then again, it might look as if I had an unfair advantage. Would the other girls be jealous and resentful? What if it worked against me? After a moment's hesitation, I came to the conclusion that any of those girls next door could also have been drumming up press to highlight their individuality, if they were keen enough. Why should I let my reservations hold me back, especially as I was also taking the risk of looking like a right fool if I didn't make it to the finals?

'Of course not, that's fine,' I replied. 'Especially if it's helping to overthrow people's stereotypes about what Miss England is like.'

What I wasn't expecting was for the crew to sit down next to me within minutes and ask what I thought my chances were. Right there, in front of all the other girls! But if that wasn't bad enough, once they were done with me, they would move on to question the rest of the contestants about how they felt competing against a soldier. The decision's made now, I ended up thinking: I've got to give it my best.

Meanwhile, we were being taken into the judging hall in groups of six to be introduced to the panel. That year the panel of judges included Georgia Horsley (the then Miss England, who I had met at the bikini shoot a few months before), some magazine editors, stylists, Calum Best and to my horror, the photographer who had taken the images of me that mysteriously ended up in the *News of the World*.

Once we were in the room, we would have to stand forward one at a time and introduce ourselves.

'Hi, my name is Kat Hodge and I am representing Tunbridge Wells,' was what I said, before smiling at the judges and taking my position in the row again. Once everyone was done, we left the room, with the judges chattering ominously from behind their big trestle table.

Things didn't get any more comfortable after that as it was up to our rooms to change into swimwear. I had long been dreading this, but was determined to stick to my guns and did so by wearing a one-piece. It was a bright red, plain number, nothing fancy at all. As I looked around the reception room where all the other girls were waiting, I saw that I was the only girl not in a bikini and some of them were in really fancy designer bikinis. My heart sank: I did wonder if I might be going home soon. Were Miss England just talking the talk when they said that it wasn't all about looks, but personality and drive as well? Had times really changed or was it still a dazzling smile and a bikini body that won votes? There was only one way to find out.

It only lasted a moment, though. I reckoned that if I were going to be judged like this, at least I'd do it on my own terms: for being me, and not for trying to look like one of the others. The waiting seemed to go on forever, however. This time, we were going in groups of only three, so the process took twice as long.

After a couple of hours it was my group's turn to enter the judging hall. We were only in there for a couple of minutes, but I hated every second of it. There we all were, lined up like last time, except now we had nothing to say for ourselves. Other girls who are not so confident with their job or their personality are often happy to be competing in a round where they do not have to speak as much, but I always felt horribly stifled when expected to express myself entirely through my physical attributes. I could feel Calum Best's gaze going up and down me as I stood there, wincing. As I stood in that room, I made the decision that the bikini round really is inexcusable: it is 100 per cent based on looks, which are something you can do so little about if you are to remain natural and healthy.

And it's just plain boring; there's no chance for you to do or say anything of interest or value about yourself, literally nothing left to be judged but the width of your hips and the curve of your chest. As I left the room, I shuddered – relieved to the core that it was over.

The evening's events were much more my style, however: dinner. I was starving by then! There was only one small problem: because we were in a health spa, the meal was... well it was dainty, to say the least. I sat there, trying to pick up a bit of seaweed with my fork, thinking, 'Is no one else hungry? Anyone? *Anyone?*' I'm sure it must have been a healthy meal, but frankly it wasn't enough for me.

The minute we were free, I used my sneakiest Army manoeuvres and escaped. Soon, I was off in my car – and not long after that, I was wolfing down a KFC Meal Deal, happy as a clam!

The next morning I woke to the soft shuffling sounds of someone else moving around in the bedroom. As I lay in bed, I got my bearings and then opened one eye, filled with terror.

Had I slept through my alarm?

My one opened eye revealed that the room was already light and my roommate up and about. She was sitting at the dressing table, furiously tweaking away at her hair.

OK, I *had* slept through my alarm. How long did I have to get ready?

We needed to be downstairs by 9am, so I had set my alarm for 7am. I took a deep breath, sat bolt upright and decided to confront my alarm clock head-on.

6.58am.

What?

'Hey, what time is it?' I asked in the most natural, breezy voice that I could muster.

'Oh hi!' said my roommate, barely cracking a smile. 'Just before seven – you need to get up if you're going to be ready in time.'

'Er, yeah,' I replied. 'How long have *you* been up?'

'Since five.'

Whoa! What had she been doing? Admittedly, she looked almost entirely ready at this point, so maybe the real question was what was she going to do now?

I got out of bed and wandered towards the shower. When I returned, about fifteen minutes later, she was sitting on the edge of the bed, looking more frantic than ever. Her hair, which had been in a perfect blow-dried and demi-waved up-do when I left the room, was now unfurling around her shoulders. Half backcombed and half hairsprayed, it was now 100 per cent dishevelled. She was gazing into her lap, sadly.

'Why did you undo your hair?' I asked. Had the first version just been a practice run? If so, she was hardcore.

'It wasn't right,' she told me. 'It just wasn't perfect. I'm going to have to start all over again.'

'Oh no, I'm sorry,' I replied while trying to give her a cheering smile but to be honest, her horror at my 'late' waking hour seemed to have made her distrust me. For the next couple of hours silence largely filled the space between us as we sat on opposite sides of the room, slowly making ourselves ready for the day. I put my hair in rollers, took my hair out of rollers and then did my usual make-up, but with my new roommate twitching around in the background, it felt as if it wasn't enough. Then I found myself stabbing away at my eyeliner, trying to perfect something I had never noticed was 'wrong' before. Ugh!

By the time we headed downstairs together there was a definite vibe of fake support. I was sick of being made to feel paranoid by her, while she seemed pretty insulted by my 'slapdash' efforts at being a beauty queen. My mind was whizzing. Only 10 girls out of the 50 there that day would make it to the finals: did I really stand a chance?

In my favour was the fact that it was the interview round that morning. All 50 of us sat in that same room next to the judging area, making polite conversation amongst ourselves for hours on end. Meanwhile, we'd be called in one by one to have our chat with the judges. Time seemed to be moving at half its usual speed, especially as I had the added pressure of the Channel 5 cameras following me. As we sat there, I could see Angie flitting in and out overseeing everything. She was constantly monitoring the situation, keeping an eye on all of us. I got the feeling that not much would get past her beady gaze: she seemed more than able to sift the prima donnas from the girls with their heads screwed on straight.

My number was 47, so I had seen almost everyone come and go before my turn. The atmosphere was getting more and more highly charged. It was like when you leave a school exam room and immediately start swapping what answers you gave and who you think did the best. I tried to block it all out and remind myself that I had faced properly tense and dangerous situations in Iraq: this was a hobby, I mustn't let it get out of hand.

Once I was finally standing in front of the judges, they watched my talent DVD. It seemed bizarre to see myself in my uniform and no make-up after the two hours that I had just spent getting ready. And then, that first question. It wasn't one that was new to me: if anything, it was a question I had been asked in disbelief several times over the past few months.

'So, are you in the actual Army?'

'Yes, of course – I wouldn't lie about it.' As ever, I tried to be firm but with a smile. Why did people always think the two were so incompatible? The next questions were not much more surprising.

'Why do you want to be Miss England?'

'What made you enter?'

'What would make you a good Miss England?'

'Why is an Army girl interested in taking part in this competition?'

By now, I had been asked these questions so many times before that I was confident and happy to talk them through it all. I felt as if I was a different girl to the one who had stood in front of them in a swimsuit the day before.

'I want to be Miss England to prove that you don't have to be drop-dead gorgeous to be a role model and to prove

143

that the definition of drop-dead gorgeous doesn't need to be a purely physical one. I want to show young girls who might have doubts about themselves that if you set your mind to something, then barely anything is impossible.

'When I first entered this competition I could barely walk properly in high heels and I had spent the last four years wearing combats to work, yet here I am now. I want to prove that the two don't need to be mutually exclusive: you can do a job like being in the Army and still be a beautiful, feminine girl.'

I paused and took a deep breath. They seemed to be smiling. The next question did catch me off-guard, though.

'If you were an animal, which one would you be?'

Of course, I had no idea what the right answer to that might be, in terms of winning the competition, so I went with the truth.

'I think I'd be a monkey. I'm cheeky and I have lots of hair!'

'And finally, if you were stuck on a desert island, what would you take with you?'

This one seemed silly: they hadn't thought it through for a girl like me.

'I'd take everything I needed to get off – a boat, a phone, some flares.'

With a gulp, I realised that most of the other girls would probably have named classic beauty essentials. Oh well, I'd told the truth and there was nothing I could do to change things now. Half an hour later we were all back in the room, lined up for the judges' announcement.

Standing there in that conference room, I looked round at all the other girls and faced a rare moment of doubt. It was a swanky hotel event room that had probably held a thousand glamorous charity events and countless dull work seminars, but to me it was the room in which I found myself thinking, 'Yeah, it might not be me after all, but I've got this far so at least I'll be able to say to my kids in years to come, "I went to the Miss England semi-finals one year."

I was proud to have – literally – stuck to my guns, though. If I didn't get through, I could still hold my head up high and I knew it wouldn't be because I had compromised my personality or beliefs. I had been myself, and if that wasn't good enough, so be it. But while I was standing on that stage listening to the results being called out, I couldn't help but feel that flicker of hope still there. And then they called my name...

Normally, I laugh at people who cry and put on a great big performance at places like the Oscars but because I wasn't expecting it, I exploded into tears. I was shaking, I couldn't move, I couldn't walk out there in front of everyone: I had won a place in the Miss England final! No one was more surprised than me. Eventually one of the other girls had to grab me and encourage me to go up onto the stage. All I could hear in my head was, 'You're going to the finals of Miss England!'

I had always known there was no point in entering the competition if I wasn't going to give it my all, but I hadn't realised the extent to which I had been keeping a lid on my emotions. Presenting a brave, composed exterior throughout the competition had suddenly turned me into a gibbering wreck – sobbing and shaking, quivering at the realisation that I was one step closer to my dream. I was embarrassed by this outburst and vowed never again to let my emotions get the better of me in this way.

I wasn't the only one who was having trouble controlling their emotions. As I scanned the room, I saw my roommate. Her face was filled with fury as she turned, avoiding the gaze of everyone else there. Most of the girls were chatting, hugging and either commiserating or congratulating each other. She left without saying a word to anyone. I made a quiet note to myself that nothing is worth that kind of misery: she had over-invested in her looks and left out her strength of character.

There were just three weeks between the semi-final and the date of the Miss England final itself in July 2008, which left me with hardly any time to get prepared. The other contestants were knee-deep in sequins as they busied themselves in selecting bespoke dresses for the final. Unable to take time off work for fittings, I had to find a suitable off-the-peg dress at the last minute. I should never have worried about that though, as it was far from being the dress itself that would make the biggest splash on the night.

One of the rounds in the final was an 'eco' round, where the outfits had to be created by the competitors and each girl would promote recycling in some way. It seemed the majority of the other competitors had interpreted this to mean vintage frocks or something of sentimental value that their mother had worn before them. I didn't have their experience, though: instead, I took the theme a little more literally and created a papier-mâché ball dress on a chicken wire frame, made entirely from old newspapers ready for recycling. Many of the news stories commemorated colleagues that my Corps had lost fighting in Iraq.

It may have been far more original than anything anyone else had come up with, but presented a problem I hadn't anticipated: the 'eco' dress was the one that the contestants were to wear for the dinner! If only someone had told me. My dress was entirely solid! It was impossible to sit on a chair at the dinner table. After a kerfuffle, one of the organisers managed to find me a little stool so I could perch on it, while the dress hooped over the top.

It was a lucky dress, however: it won me the round and meant that I was placed fourth in Miss England 2008. The winner was Laura Coleman, who is now one of my best friends. Her mum and nan were both beauty queens and she's a gorgeous size 12, so it just goes to show that you can be curvy and still win Miss England!

Though I had done better than I ever anticipated, I wasn't Miss England. I thought the adventure was over. It was an extraordinary experience, but one I never expected to have again. The next morning, I went back to normality: I put my combats and boots back on and got on with Army life.

CHAPTER SEVEN

A SECOND CHANCE – MISS ENGLAND 2009

I T TURNS out that some dreams don't die that easily. I thought I was heading back to life in the barracks: hair scraped back, combats on and a regiment of soldiers for company. Once again, glamour was going to be an occasional weekend-only treat.

Then, in March 2009 things changed. I was at home watching television and looking pretty glamorous, I might add: pyjamas, massive socks, no make-up, the works... when I flipped open my laptop to check my emails. There was an automatically generated newsletter from the Miss England website administrators. The rules stated that as I had won a section at last year's competition, I would automatically be placed in the semi-finals of Miss England 2009, should I choose to enter.

'Should I choose to enter...' Tempting, but did I really

want to put myself through all of that again – the work, the stress, the travel? And after all, I had had a great time last year: I was really happy with the position I'd achieved and I didn't want to enter a second time and do worse. Plus, I didn't think I'd be able to win anyway, so what was the point if I wasn't going to go after the big prize?

But, as I had my laptop right there in front of me, I thought I might as well log on to Facebook while I was thinking about it. After all, I had fully connected with my old Army mates over the last few months, so it seemed about time to catch up with some of my pageant pals. I already had messages from some of the other girls I'd met last year. Luckily, it wasn't the scary competitive girls that I'd heard from, but the nice girls who had become friends.

'Are you going to re-enter?'

'What do you reckon? We could do it all together!'

'It would be so good to hang out with each other again...'

'But is it worth it? There's no way I'd win.'

'Well, all the recent winners have won in the second year that they took part...'

They all seemed to be thinking the same as I was: it would be fun to see each other again, but did we need the hassle?

What have I got to lose? I started to think to myself. This year, the answer really was only time: I didn't have much to spare. I knew that it wouldn't cost me much to compete because as a finalist from the year before I had already been approached by dress companies, who had said they would happily provide me with gowns as sponsorship. And I needed smart dresses for work from time to time as the Sergeants' Mess (a sort of Armed Forces members' club) had formal dinners at least two or three times a year that we had to attend, so any sponsored dresses would get a bit of proper use beyond the world of the pageants and it wouldn't be a total waste.

The temptation was getting stronger.

As all girls know, sometimes the best bit of a night out is the getting ready. You know what it's like: the week before, you're in the Topshop changing rooms, leaning up against your handbag and your rumpled jeans, trying to take a picture on your phone to text to your mates for an opinion. Then you're all in a bedroom together – music on the stereo, glasses of wine on the go, doing each other's hair and lending accessories to get the perfect look. Sometimes the night that follows can be a bit of a letdown, but that girly time in the run-up rarely is.

And that's what taking part in pageants is like. Maybe not the first one or two when you're still getting to know people, but I knew this year it would be just like one big run-up to a great night out. After several months in my combats and no make-up, I really missed the girls and the girliness.

So in the end it came down to a social decision rather than a competitive one. Having got as far as I did last time, I decided that I didn't have any expectations and I would enter again as a hobby – a bit of a girly break after nine months of Army life and a chance to catch up with all the friends I'd made.

I applied online and the wheels swung back into motion: I couldn't enter Miss Tunbridge Wells for a second time as that was the heat I'd won the year before. However, the rules stated that if you had family in other regions then you were eligible to enter in them. I had family in Derby, so that was where I applied. Shortly afterwards, I went up there for a pageant. While I was enjoying being back in the world of frocks and falsies, I did feel a bit out of place in Derby. After all, I was a bit out of place! I hadn't grown up there and it didn't seem quite right that that was the route I was taking to Miss England. Also, it was very obvious that I wasn't a local because of my accent and the judges wasted no time in letting me know that I was placed second in the competition rather than first because I wasn't a girl who could really represent Derby to the nation. Fair enough, I hadn't grown up there and talking to me you'd know I'm not a Northern lass: I was glad that someone local won. It was time for Plan B.

This entailed the Miss Every Model heats. *Every Model* is the modelling industry's trade magazine, representing and reporting on the industry. They have an annual pageant themselves, which allocates the winner a place in the grand final of Miss England. It's a tough one though, because most of the girls who enter are already modelling professionals and the selection is from all over the country.

But it was worth a shot: as I had already decided, what did I really have to lose?

The first stage involved a photographic shoot in Islington for all of the entrants and the images that were taken and put up on their website were then used for the text vote. When I logged on a week after the shoot to see the results, I frowned at my screen. All the other girls were represented by stunning headshots taken that day, but for me they were using a full-length image.

Oh Kat, clearly you didn't take a good enough headshot, I thought. You don't have a hope in hell of winning this one.

I reminded myself that I was in it just for fun and the next weekend I headed up to Stanford near Peterborough, ready for the pageant itself. The email that had been sent the day before reminded me sternly that we were to go there with strictly no make-up or hairstyles done. If we arrived with any product on our face or hair then we would be instructed to remove it immediately before being permitted to take part in the pageant. Harsh... especially when I arrived and saw how utterly gorgeous so many of the professional models there were.

Half an hour later, I was on more familiar ground, though. All of the contestants were in a big conference room in the hotel, the tables pushed back around the sides of the room and several garment rails wheeled in and positioned in key areas. I put my bags down and scanned the scene before me. Here I was again and all of the familiar faces were there, too.

Now I'm not talking about specific girls but the archetypes that are there at every pageant. Let me talk you through them, in case you ever find yourself among us.

Type 1 – The Show-off. A pageant isn't a pageant without the 'Show-off'. She wants to win, but most of all she likes the opportunity to prance about seeking attention. You just know that this is all she has talked about to her friends for weeks. She thinks she's Lily Cole and behaves as if she's Naomi Campbell. This girl can be found in the most central position in the room, shaking out her dress. It's worth thousands and she'll be the first to let you know. In fact, she will stand in the middle of the room brushing it out until someone walks by and compliments her on it.

Type 2 – Mummy's Little Girl. I always feel sorry for 'Mummy's Little Girl', but you can't help wishing she'd simply stand up for herself a bit more. She's rarely alone – her mother is always inches away. Even when the pageant organisers try to keep her out of the way, she'll find a way to rush back to her little princess's side. ('Oh, your inhaler!', 'Here, your ID!' Whatever...) Mummy is clearly living out her shattered dreams through her daughter, who looks nervous and is a sickly pale beneath the foundation. Meanwhile, Mummy is in tight leather trousers and rigid pin-curled hair. They've been the same double act for over ten years now and the big prize is surely just round the corner.

Type 3 – Miss World Peace. The girl who lives up to the

pageant cliché almost more than any other – she pretends that she's only interested in the charity element, but secretly she'd tread on the back of your gown in a heartbeat if she thought it would help her chances of winning. She constantly declares that she doesn't care who wins, as long as she can raise the profile of her chosen charity. Meanwhile, a careful glance will show that as she bends over into her bag, she is slathering her teeth in Vaseline to achieve the glossiest smile in the room. If she loves charity so much, why has she chosen to be a full-time pageant princess for the last three years instead of getting a job with one? And why is she so off-hand with the newer, less-confident girls? Oh, how we wish she'd just admit that she likes nail polish and sequins as much as the rest of us.

My eyes scanned the rest of the room. I knew there would be some representatives of the fourth group in there somewhere. After all, that was my group and to be fair, we did make up the bulk of the girls. And there she was.

Type 4 – The Normal Girl. She looks like the kind of girl you might want to go out with for the night. Someone who would lend you her lipstick and hold your hair back if you got too drunk, but not someone who would flash her most low-cut top in front of your boyfriend or ignore you when you needed a mate but she needed a haircut. Distinguishing characteristics are food in her bag and a smile on her face. I breathed a sigh of relief every time I saw one.

On this occasion 'The Normal Girl' was a girl called Toni and thank God, I found her. During the morning, we had rehearsals and were informed that it was the bikini round straight after lunch. Lunch consisted of some trays of sandwiches that were brought into the room where we were changing. Toni and I could tell that we were among professional models as a handful of them started to freak out about being bloated for the bikini round.

In my opinion, if you're a normal healthy weight, eating a sandwich isn't really going to show that much on you. It's only someone who is already gaunt who might end up looking a bit bloated after a small meal. And this was a situation that I decided to use to my advantage: Toni and I took one look at the manky sandwiches, which didn't even seem that filling, and decided to go and order some food for ourselves.

Twenty minutes later we could sense some of the others rolling their eyes in horror as we tucked into cheesy chips at the bar, but we didn't care. At least we didn't feel faint during the bikini round.

Even though I never stopped being a fan of food, there were a few other tricks and tips which I had learned from 2008 that I was glad to know about this time. I had learned how to do my make-up much more professionally – I'd pencil in my eyebrows to draw attention to my eyes, and I'd use a highlighting cream on my cheeks – and I'd finally mastered the art of walking gracefully on stage after years spent marching on parade grounds. Also, I had found out from other girls that a slick of Vaseline down the front of your shins really does add a bit of shine and slims your legs, but I'd resisted the Vaseline-on-the-teeth trick, although the rumours you hear about other girls doing it are 100 per cent true. It must taste grotesque!

But the one that sounds the most crazy but works the best is the hairspray-bum. I kid you not! For girls who feel horribly self-conscious about going on stage in the swimwear round, the niftiest trick to keeping your bikini bottom from riding up your... er... bottom, is to spray both with hairspray. It keeps the fabric – and your dignity – in place.

Then there are the tricks that just don't work: the one so many girls think that they have fooled everyone with is plain old lying. On entry forms you always have to give your height, as for a few of the rounds we are positioned in height order. I am 5ft 9in and I always put my real height. Looking at the line-ups, it's really very obvious who has been economical with the truth. Every now and then, there's a big height dip where someone has awarded themselves a couple of extra inches in the hope that no one else will notice. Well, we do!

The rounds in this particular pageant were eveningwear, swimwear and the fashion round, for which we had to select an outfit of our choice 'to go out in'. Having that bit of experience had taught me to choose an outfit that would make me stand out and so for the fashion round I chose to interpret the suggestion as referring to my outdoors job rather than a social occasion: I wore my hair up in a regulation bun with my Army uniform. I was back on familiar ground!

When we came to the eveningwear round, the girl walking on stage in front of me was wearing a long, narrow satin dress. It was the kind of design that stops you from being able to open your feet more than a tiny step apart. She was walking like a stressed-out penguin and almost inevitably, when we came to the steps by the side of the stage she tripped and fell. Immediately I helped her up, as that's the kind of mistake that I had spent all of the previous year's competition moments away from making.

I got through to the top ten of the fashion round, which meant that I was interviewed on stage, as was the girl before me who had tripped. Having answered the usual batch of questions about being in the Army before, I felt confident and happy talking to the judges while I was up there. However, the first-timer was completely over-whelmed. She had obviously not got over the horrors of her trip and when the judges asked her the first question she just stood there, her jaw gaping open, unable to say anything. It was a total tumbleweed moment. Eventually I grabbed her hand and said: 'Come on, you can talk! Just let me them know what you think.' I continued to hold her hand and eventually she perked up a bit.

When the time came to announce the winners I looked across the row and picked out the girls who I thought would come first and second. Moments later, they were awarded second and third place. Mentally, I was already packing my bag when suddenly I heard the presenter's voice booming out.

'And the winner is… Kat Hodge!'

I was stunned. But it seemed that Miss Every Model had also realised that a bit of personality and a dash of kindness were worth as much as perfect hair and make-up. As I walked on stage to collect my flowers, Stevie Wonder's 'Isn't She Lovely' was blasting out of the sound system, just about managing to drown out the noise of my heart thundering with pride. Oh my God, I'm in the Miss England finals again…

Before tackling the finals, I had one extra treat in store. Well, it was supposed to be a treat but I confess it was a bit of an emotional rollercoaster: my first high-end photo shoot. As part of the prize for winning Miss Every Model, I was awarded a day of professional hair, make-up and styling, then a high fashion shoot for the front cover of *Every Model* magazine. The photographic studio was in Islington and even though everyone there was absolutely lovely, I was quickly overwhelmed with a sense of 'Toto, we're not in Kansas any more…'

The minute I arrived, the team took one look at my face and decided instead of the usual beauty queen look that I go for – big eyes, big lips and long eyelashes – I should have a 'stripped-back' look. Eek! It's one thing to have no make-up on if you're on exercise or driving a Snatch vehicle, but stripped back for a photo shoot?

I was also used to having classic glossy hair, but this time the hairstylist backcombed it to within an inch of my life while I was having my deathly pale lipstick applied. As for the clothes, they were amazing but they weren't very me. I was in *Sex and the City*-style frocks, leather gloves, huge tutus, with a tiara perched on the side of my head. It was all very Taylor Momsen – they were calling me a 'rock princess'.

As I walked into the studio and out in front of the camera, the photographer appeared. He was a classic East London fashionista type. If he were cast as a trendy snapper in a sitcom, people would say it was too much! With his little goatee and tiny pork-pie hat perched on top of an expensive-looking haircut, it was all I could do not to get the giggles.

'Right, darling,' he told me, as I walked onto the set. 'I want to see you fierce. Angry. It's you against the music.'

'OK,' I replied, and stood there waiting for the music that I was 'against'. I glanced around, trying to spot some speakers.

Silence. A room full of intense stylists was staring at me, with their arms crossed and tiny frowns on their faces. I looked back, expectantly.

It turned out there was no music: it was just an expression that the photographer had decided to use. That set the tone for the rest of the shoot. I'm glad I did it, but all day I was overwhelmed by a sense of it just not being my thing. Once I'd been 'against the music', then I was a 'broken-down doll', like on *America's Next Top Model*, then I was 'looking fierce' while lying on the floor. I hate to say it, but I actually looked more as if I'd just been run over than anything else.

What am I doing here? I wondered to myself, as the shutter clicked away. Meanwhile, the photographer continued to talk at me.

'Yeah, yeah, this is really great. We're getting it, we're getting it! We *so* got it!' he declared.

What are you talking about?

'The music is really taking you away now, isn't it? Yeah, you just don't care, the music has got you now!'

But there is no music.

'Angry now, I want to see real anger... *Yes*!'

But I didn't move my face – I was just thinking about how to look angry.

'Now, pick up your shoes. Carry them loosely. I want you look like you've just come home at six in the morning.'

You're going to make me look like those government ads against drinking. That's not a beauty-queen look...

'Grab the wall, use the set and make it yours!'

So I grabbed hold of some of the unfurled wallpaper dangling from the ceiling of the artfully distressed set. I didn't realise it was as loose as it was and suddenly swung forward like a drunk, startled monkey.

What on earth were those pictures going to look like?

'Now we want you against the music. Fight the music!'

Do you know what, I've fought bigger enemies than music, mate! When you're in the bottom of a vehicle with an Iraqi holding your own weapon to your face, that's a fight.

'Wow, you *are* dangerous!'

Yes, yes, I can be.

They were all lovely people, but everyone seemed to be taking fashion much, much more seriously than I ever could. By the end of the day I was craving to get back to work and roll around in some mud with a bunch of blokey men. In the end, the photographs themselves were not so bad and for me, it was great profile that I was on the cover of *Every Model*, which was displayed at the Miss England finals. What an amazing opportunity! It's just that I look really unhappy in them and that's not my thing. I am not an 'edgy' person, which is fine by me!

After that shoot there were only two months until the Miss England finals. It wasn't long, but the huge difference was that year, I knew just what I was doing. I knew what to get, where to get it, how much to practise and most importantly, I decided to save time by using the same talent DVD as the year before. The good old rifle drill was back! All I really had to do was organise an outfit to arrive in, get a pageant dress for the formal wear round and sort out my eco-wear.

My priority in each case was to stand out: I was never going to be the most beautiful girl in the room, but I had every chance of looking like the most interesting or the most confident one so I would play to my strengths and use that. I knew that most of the girls wore smart dresses to arrive in. Registration and the first couple of rounds would be done in outfits of our choice, so it was an important look. In 2008, I had made the same decision as most: an office-wear style skirt and top. That year, I stuck to my new theme of standing out and with the bit of extra confidence the high-fashion shoot had given me, I decided to wear trousers. They sound disgusting – sky blue and white, high-waisted, pinstripe pants. I nearly didn't even bother trying them on, but I'm so glad I did. With them, I wore a white shirt with enormous shoulders and I do admit that I looked a little like Krystle Carrington, but I stood out! When I walked into the room, I felt like Miss England.

The pageant dress I already had – it was red and backless. Perfect.

As for the dress for the eco round, the previous year I had learned a valuable practical lesson: best if you can sit down in it! This time we were given the 1970s as a theme. I had an idea of what I wanted to wear, but it involved a slightly awkward call to the Adjutant General Corps Museum.

'Er, hi... Do you have any uniforms for women, from the 1970s?'

'Yes, we do. We don't have them on display at the moment, though.'

'Oh, that's OK. That's um, a bit better actually.'

'Rii-iight. What is it that you actually want?'

'Well, I wondering if I could borrow one.'

'I'm afraid I will have to ask why.'

'To wear for the finals of Miss England.'

They certainly weren't expecting that, but in the end they were lovely about it and lent me a seriously funky outfit. I drove all the way to Winchester to pick it up and when I saw the colours, my jaw dropped. For military uniform, it was actually rather weird. It was still smart, but it was a bright blue straight, knee-length skirt and matching jacket with a mint green shirt and a jaunty peaked cap. I looked like a psychedelic airhostess, especially as there was heavy gold braiding on the lapels and over the shoulders. Like I said, it was funky stuff!

The final was held at the Hilton London Metropole on 20 July 2009. When the date rolled around, I had my outfits ready and was relaxed about taking part. As I walked through the big gold swing doors to the hotel, the first person I saw was the recent Miss England, Georgia Horsley – the girl with whom I had done the Miss England bikini shoot, the year before.

'Wow, Kat, you look great!' was the first thing she said to me when she saw my risky blue trouser outfit. It gave me just the buzz I needed as I walked up to the registration area.

Within ten minutes of all of us registering we were ushered in for the Helen E Award for Best Face. Helen E wais the cosmetics brand sponsoring the competition and this was a tough round as there is only so much you can do about your face, if you are used to getting by on personality! The winner of that round was Rachel Christie, one of the girls I had become friendly with that year. She was Olympic star Linford's niece and I liked the fact that she had a bit of feistiness and wasn't just another blonde goddess: she had personality and goals beyond the pageant world as she was aiming for the 2012 Olympics. I was pleased for Rachel, and surprised myself by coming second.

Next up was the Best Hair. This round is judged not on any particular style that we were wearing, but the cut and condition of our actual hair. Extensions are allowed, although you have to be wearing them as actual hair, not the weird ratty situation that Britney can sometimes have going on!

The rest of the day was spent in rehearsals for the big 'pageanty' final the next night. It was so much more fun than the previous year as I was relaxed and chatting with all the girls, everything seemed easier. Some of the first-timers were asking my advice and I couldn't believe that that had been me only a year ago. Maybe I got a little too relaxed, though as I entirely lost track of time and ended up running very late for the evening dinner. I don't know how it happened, but I'd only left myself with ten minutes to get ready for the opening gala dinner of Miss England! I was wearing my vintage Army uniform and some mascara I'd put on in the hotel lift.

Other girls had gone all out for the recycling round and were wearing dresses made of seventies' records and things like that. As I scanned the room, I realised the stakes had certainly been raised that year. I felt especially self-conscious as the evening wore on and I realised that my uniform was 1970s to perfection – down to the stinking mothball smell! It couldn't be washed in case the process subjected the vintage fabric and detailing to too much wear and tear, but after being worn for twenty minutes, everyone in the room could tell.

The other competitors, and my friends and family who had all come to wish me well could hardly bear to go near me while I was wearing my costume – it was so stinky. For me, it had to be endured, though. As I walked onto the stage for my moment in the spotlight, I thought I just have to admit it. The pong was unavoidable and I didn't want anyone thinking it was my personal hygiene standards. 'This is an original 1970s uniform complete with matching smell,' I announced. The host had a whiff and confirmed to the audience that yes, he could verify its authenticity even if it wasn't the most pleasant task of his evening.

That night they also showed the talent DVDs. Mine was about ninth out of the ten shown. I was absolutely convinced that the winner would be Anna Watts, Miss Hertfordshire, who had a DVD of her singing Duffy's 'Warwick Avenue'. OK, I know that the cliché of a pageant girl singing brings to mind Katie Price's Eurovision attempts, but Anna really was sensational. She was also a lovely girl, as was obvious from her stage interview.

I enjoyed my own interview – it consisted mostly of questions I'd answered before and like talking about. Up on stage, I said that I was keen to show that Army girls aren't all butch, humourless, wannabe men and that I wanted to bring something more than just plastic beauty to the pageant world. I was happy chatting – if anything, I worried that I was too relaxed and hadn't tried hard enough. My fears were proved unfounded, however, when I heard them announce my name as winner. What a perfect way to end the evening!

The next day flew by: I had decided to take part for the experience and the glamour as much as anything that year, so I revelled in every false eyelash and every moment on the catwalk. There weren't many falsies first thing that morning, though: in fact, there was no make-up at all. We were told to be barefaced and arrive downstairs with our hair scraped back into high ponytails. Some girls were completely freaked out by this, but luckily my years of working in an environment that didn't allow make-up served me well: you have to be confident in your own skin.

The reason for our stripped-back hair and pared-down make-up was that the fashion round was supposed to demonstrate that we could show off a dress without seeking attention ourselves. Fashion students from around the country created all the gowns. I had collected mine from Liverpool and was almost as shocked when I saw it as when I got a whiff of my vintage uniform. It had a wide black belt and enormous full-length tutu skirt, with an almost entirely transparent white top. It barely covered my boobs! I decided to wear a white bikini beneath it. There are some things I'm never going to do in the name of glamour.

Walking down the catwalk in the dress was quite an effort, too. The skirts were so long and so thick, I had to almost do a full can-can underneath them to make enough room to actually move my feet, one in front of the other! It was designed to represent a swan on a lake. Things were serene up top but beneath the skirts, it was chaos. Added to the problem was the fact that we were walking to Lady Gaga's 'Pokerface', which is a fast song. I was almost at a canter, as Gaga sang on and on about her P-p-p-p-okerface.

Despite – or maybe because of – the effort I had had to make to stay upright on the catwalk, I won that round as well. I was pleased, but never 100 per cent surprised when I did well on rounds where I had a chance to talk about my unusual career as I was always aware that it was good to sound different, to stand out. But it was a surprising boost when I shone in the fashion round as it meant I wasn't entirely an oddity: I was actually capable of being a tomboy with a hectic job as well as a beautiful girl with something to say for herself.

Consequently, while we were having our hair and make-up done, I started to let myself believe that maybe I did have a chance of winning Miss England after all. The successes I'd had in earlier rounds meant that I had the relief of knowing I was in the top 15, but it wasn't all good news: the top 15 girls are the ones expected to take part in the swimsuit round! That year, you were simply handed your outfit as you went backstage – there was no choice, no arguing and therefore no lying about what size you might be. Thankfully, I was one of the contestants given a one-piece to wear. Maybe Miss England really did think beauty was about more than doing the catwalk in a bikini.

For the final round, I wore a gorgeous red dress. We did our interviews on the stage and then all 15 of us were ushered backstage, waiting to hear the announcement of the final results. They only announced the top three, so I knew that if I heard my name called at all, I would have done better than last year's fourth place. They announced third place, then left a huge pause. It was a proper *X Factor*-style moment of tension – one of those horrible pauses when everyone is searching everyone else's face for some kind of clue as to what they're thinking. Meanwhile, everyone is equally keen not to catch anyone else's eye in case it gives too much away. The silence seemed to go on forever: the stage lights started to feel hotter, my face felt as if it was going red beneath the make-up and the moment of truth didn't seem to be drawing any nearer. Then... my name! I had come second. *Me*!

It was such a weird experience: I had just come second in Miss England! I couldn't believe that I had gone back for a second time and had done even better than the year before. I'd only done it for fun and yet I had ended up so much better. But still, there was a tiny nagging voice in my mind: 'Second... that's so close to first. How come you didn't make it? What more could you have done? What a shame...'

Regardless of any frustration I felt about coming so close to being Miss England, I was genuinely pleased for the winner Rachel Christie, who had also been a competitor the year before and had become a close friend of mine. She had been on a real journey in the competition. In 2008, she had had no confidence and looked totally different but she had a great story and lots of determination. Like me, she wanted more than just Miss England: she was a professional heptathlete who was aiming for a place in the 2012 Olympics. Rachel was also the first black Miss England and she won it by being herself, not pretending to be an old-fashioned pageant princess. (She does look as if she's gliding when she walks, though – it's incredible!) As she sat on the throne, I whispered to her: 'I told you you'd win!' and gave her a huge grin. She couldn't speak: she was so overwhelmed by the moment.

Meanwhile, the other person who became rather too caught up in it all was my dad. Because of the massive pause that the presenter had left between announcing second and first place, he had thought that I'd actually come first and he came rushing onto the stage to congratulate me. The day before, he'd given me such a big lecture – I couldn't believe it when he came bouncing up to me, clapping like a maniac. Only twenty-four hours earlier, it had all been: 'Don't get too excited. You probably won't win and you need to know that that doesn't matter anyway.' Now look at him! After realising his mistake, he went crimson with embarrassment. What else are dads for?

The following two or three hours were a very strange experience for me. I was struck by the fact that (apart from my dad!) no one really congratulated me on coming second in the competition. No one mentioned what an achievement it was for a girl like me. All I heard was 'Are you gutted?', 'You were so close!', 'How annoyed are you?', 'Are you OK?' I wanted to tell them to back off and stop spoiling the genuine excitement I felt that I had been placed second.

While we were having the winners' photographs taken, I could feel the adrenaline draining from my body and I started to feel overwhelmed with tiredness. I could hear the fun and hubbub of the party going on elsewhere in the hotel for about two hours while we were in front of the cameras and I was sad to be missing it. By the time I got there, I was so exhausted that I only stayed for about half an hour and then went up to my room. The minute my head hit the pillow, I was sound asleep.

When I woke up the next morning, I had two rather nice surprises waiting for me: I was invited downstairs to collect my prizes for coming second, which were a set of suitcases, cosmetics, accessories and all sorts. And I had been asked to go on *GMTV* for a third appearance! I was the most chuffed I have ever been to be asked: normally, the day after Miss England, no one gives a stuff about the girl who comes second but this time the media were making a story out of us both being exceptional girls. People were interested in seeing us as a pair, which was a great feeling of achievement.

Rachel and I went on to do several media interviews

together as the press was taken with the modern image of Miss England – a soldier and a future Olympic athlete. Knowing this was a temporary situation and that it was a great chance for the Army to promote its women and the role they did, the military bosses were very supportive about me giving media interviews. I wasn't asked to talk about my life beyond the Army or Miss England, so I don't know how the bosses would have felt had I started to do tacky 'at home' photo spreads or give detailed interviews that broke Army confidentiality about military operations, but I imagine their support would have vanished pretty quickly. As it was, I was proud to be out there in my uniform, representing the brave and hard-working Forces women, who are rarely given a voice in the media.

A week later I was approached by the La Senza lingerie chain to be the face of their stores. With a plan up my sleeve, I agreed to the shoot in principle. I decided to try my hand and suggest to them that I would do it on one condition: that they agreed to give all serving members of the Forces a 15 per cent discount. No disrespect, but students are offered discounts in countless stores, while members of the Armed Forces are rarely treated the same. When you've been in Army uniform for a while, you want to have something nice on the rest of the time and it's important to Army girls to still feel feminine. It's one of those issues that you don't really think of unless you've had experience of it – after weeks in sandy tents in Iraq, I was dying to wear some glamorous undies and the idea of being able to help others who must feel the same was a real sticking point for me. However, my determination served me well and the chain agreed to my terms.

There was no doubt I was excited about getting a major modelling job outside the world of pageants, but I was definitely also anxious about the shoot itself. While not exactly raunchy, it was still underwear: having rejected the bikini option twice in the competition and had my fingers burned at that first Miss England bikini shoot, this time I was going to be 100 per cent sure that I maintained control of my image.

People have asked me why I would model in my underwear if I hate the swimsuit round of the competition so much. The answer is simple: no one forced me to do the La Senza shoot. It was offered to me, and I saw an opportunity to change the image of girls in the Armed Forces and to strike a deal for a Forces discount. But the bikini rounds of Miss England were compulsory, and at a time when the organisers stated that they were taking personality and attitude into comparison as well, it seemed utterly irrelevant. If you do photographs for lads' mags, it's obvious that it's your body you are promoting, not the outfit you're wearing but with La Senza, it really is about the underwear as those images are aimed at girls.

The La Senza shoot nearly didn't happen though, as it was scheduled to take place the day after I had an operation on my arm. I was due to have surgery on the ligaments in my wrist and would have my arm in plaster. There was no point in trying to hide it from the team at La Senza – after all, there are no sleeves on an underwear shoot! In the end I arranged to have a temporary cast that I could remove briefly on the day. It wasn't my dream to be doing my one and only underwear shoot with one arm hanging limply by my side, but I had faced bigger challenges and decided to make the best of it.

Usually it is big celebrities who model for La Senza and I was understandably really nervous when I turned up. I needn't have worried, though. The team, which included Lisa Eldridge from *10 Years Younger*, who regularly works on *Vogue* shoots, was incredibly professional and quickly put me at ease.

They were positive, professional women who under-stood that these would be images for making women want to look their best in their knickers, rather than frightening them by showing them someone who looked like an inaccessible, sexy robot woman. Rather than exposed, the team made me feel great about myself: they started me 'on the baby slopes' by shooting me in some of the pyjamas first and soon the friendly atmosphere had me relaxed in some of the lovely underwear sets.

The experience also really made me think about the art involved in professional shoots – the lighting, make-up and attention to angles and details. Up until this point, most of my modelling had been live and now I realised how much can be achieved by slick professionalism. You open a magazine and your instinct is to think, 'Wow, I'd love to look like that girl' but even she doesn't look like that girl, trust me!

Around this time I started to receive a flood of emails and Facebook messages from young girls who had secretly been thinking about going into the Army, but felt they didn't have anyone to talk to about it, or thought they were too girly to make it. I always tried to reply to them all, as I still do. Seeing that I was 'normal' had convinced them they might have a chance after all and my ambition was to break down the prejudices which have developed around both Miss England and the Army. And while I was just starting to realise the possibilities of my new profile, I received the biggest news of all...

CHAPTER EIGHT

MISS ENGLAND, AT LAST!

WITH RENEWED confidence after Miss England and the La Senza shoots, I went back to work. Though I really felt I had done my bit to represent the Army in a positive way, I was also glad to be back at work and getting into the swing of things again. I kept in touch with the girls from Miss England and popped onto the Facebook page from time to time to check out the news, but I felt happy with what I'd achieved and didn't regret re-entering. Meanwhile, I was promoted in the autumn and had a nice pay rise on the way. All was good for Corporal Hodge – I was getting on with life!

But life changed one November day, when I came in from training. I'd been outside and returned to the changing room freezing cold and covered in mud, with the sweat drying on me, fingers numb. I glanced at my mobile in my kit bag and saw that I had six missed calls and three voicemails. I'd only been out an hour or so. Then I noticed that they were all from the Miss England office. What on earth...?

My first thought was to wonder what I might have done wrong. What could the worst-case scenario be? I really couldn't think of one so I assumed that it was maybe something to do with some of the press I had done with Rachel Christie, or perhaps a matter concerning La Senza.

With fumbling fingers, I pressed 'Voicemail' and listened. The first message was a simple one: 'Hi Kat, it's Angie from Miss England here. Could you give me a call back when you get a chance? Hope all's well.'

The second one was a bit more urgent: 'Hi Kat, it's Angie again. Could you give me a call back as soon as possible? I'd really like to talk to you in the next hour or so. Thanks.'

Then, things were getting a little frantic: 'Hi Kat, I'm sorry to hound you like this. It's Angie. We really do need you to call back as soon as you get these messages. Please. Thanks, speak soon.'

I was starting to feel shivery, with both cold and panic. Hugging myself to try and keep warm, I called Angie straight back.

'Hi Angie, it's Kat. I've just got your voicemails. Is everything OK?'

'Oh hi, thanks so much for calling back! Yes, things are

fine, but we've got a bit of news. I think I need you might need to sit down first...'

'Um, OK. What's happened?' I perched on the edge of the bench in the changing room, gripping the phone tightly in one hand and fretfully twiddling the zip of my hoodie with the other.

'This can't get out to anyone yet but you need to know. Is there any chance you could take five and half weeks off work, starting tomorrow?'

'What job is this?' I asked, starting to freak out a bit. I watched my hand frantically yanking the zipper of my hoodie up and down one side.

'Well, if you were able to take that time off, we'd like you to go to Miss World in 48 hours' time. But you can't tell anyone about this.'

The world suddenly seemed to slow down. They wanted *me* to go to Miss World? I wasn't Miss England, I was Corporal Hodge again... What was going on?

'You might want to go and take a look at today's papers,' said Angie. 'Rachel is being dethroned. And as you were runner up, you will now become Miss England – if you accept, of course. And we would love you to represent us at Miss World.'

I glanced at myself in one of the changing-room mirrors. Sweaty hair was sticking to my head, my cheeks were still ruddy from running around outside; there were mud splatters all over my feet and lower legs, even a bit on one of my ears. This was not what Miss England looked like!

But then perhaps the administrators had been true to their word: the prize was about personality and how you carried yourself, after all. My head was spinning.

It turned out that Rachel Christie had been involved in a fight at a club and had been arrested. At the time she was dating one of the Gladiators, who competed under the name 'Tornado' but was actually called David Macintosh. He used to be in the Marines and was an all-round tough guy. While they had been out that Tuesday night, his ex-girlfriend (who happened to be Miss Manchester) had come up to them and the conversation turned into some kind of fight. I wasn't there, and I have never got to know the ins and outs of it, but Rachel was on bail and the story had hit the press. There was no question that she could go across the globe to compete in Miss World now.

'Oh Angie, that's incredible, but I just don't know if I'll be allowed to. I have the leave, but I don't know if I can just take off from work like that. I'll have to check.'

I knew that I could ask, but I was almost entirely sure that there would be no way I could do this. It was one thing for the Army to be supportive about me being at my desk an hour or two later because I'd been out promoting the Armed Forces, but five weeks of work in South Africa was rather a different kettle of fish.

'If you would, Kat, this is a really urgent situation. The press don't know that Rachel has been dethroned and we are trying to keep that news quiet until we have a new Miss England.'

It struck me that the Miss England office now needed me: they were offering me the dream, but they were also asking a huge favour. My career could depend on this, so I needed to tread carefully.

'I'll do my best, I really will, but we've got a huge inspection coming up at work and we've been told we can't take any time off at the moment. It's really unlikely.'

'I understand, but please just check?'

'I will, of course I will. Is it OK if I call you back in a couple of hours? I will go and speak to my boss but I can't imagine I'll get a definite decision very quickly.'

'Of course, speak to you soon.'

I then had the quickest shower of all time. My mind was buzzing. It seemed bizarre that I was being offered something I had dreamed of for so long, but that there were no congratulations or celebrations, just an uncanny sense of urgency.

The steely streak of determination in me really wanted to see if I could make this happen, but I was convinced that the Army just wouldn't let me swan off for so long. It seemed like a totally impossible dream. But then so too had many things before – I had learned that it's worth giving it your best shot every single time.

I didn't want to strut into my commanding officer's office and announce: 'Hey! I'm Miss England!' Experience had taught me to be a little more measured than that. I decided to go to my immediate boss, Major Clare Hudson, first. As I scurried off to try and find her, I was running through what I would say to her in my head. I must have looked a bit flustered by the time I actually did find her.

'Are you all right, Corporal Hodge?' she asked, as soon as she saw me. 'You look a bit panicked.'

'Yes, I've, um, had a bit of a phone call...'

'Right. Well, you'd better step into my office.'

And I followed her in. Major Hudson had replaced Captain Sole, the boss I had spoken to about my photographs in the *News of the World*. I had never really discussed Miss England with her, so I was going in cold. It was a bit uncomfortable having to describe the situation from the beginning. After all, she had only ever seen me as Corporal Hodge. I could see the curiosity flicker across her face as I explained. Eventually, and after a fair amount of babbling, I reached the crux of the matter.

'So, Rachel has had to stand down and the Miss England office has asked if I can step up to become Miss England. The only thing is that means I have to go to Miss World tomorrow for five weeks.'

Oh yeah, that shouldn't be a problem, I thought. Who hasn't asked for over a month off work to swan off to Miss World? I've got no chance!

'Right,' she said, frowning to herself. There was a moment's silence. 'How much annual leave do you have left? Let's think about that first.'

I had the exact amount needed, to the day. Unbelievable. I was frantically trying to find a way to say to her: 'Do you understand that they need me to leave *tomorrow*? You can't just put this to the bottom of your in-tray and have a little think about it.' Maybe my jiggling legs gave that impression.

'OK. Leave this with me,' she said. 'I'm going to have to go and talk to the Commanding Officer. It's going to be a huge thing press-wise so we'll have to get it cleared. It isn't something that can be decided in-house, by either Colonel Creasy or myself. Please could you let me know this Angie's number?'

'Thank you, ma'am, yes, here's the number.' I shoved my phone screen in front of her so that she could write it down. It actually seemed as if there might be a chance after all. Suddenly what had appeared to be an amazing but unlikely opportunity looked like it might actually be within my grasp.

'Thank you again, ma'am. I'm so sorry about this, ma'am,' was all I think of to say as I scurried out of her office.

I went to try and find my friends as fast as possible and together we rushed to the shops to buy the papers. What had been reported about Rachel and the fight? I was amazed to see it really was a big story in several of the papers, and reading about it only made me feel even more anxious that such important phone calls were going on about my future but I could do nothing more to influence the outcome.

Only ten minutes later I was called to Colonel Creasey's office. Once more, I was standing in front of him with another bizarre request.

'So, Corporal Hodge, here we are again,' he said with a smile. 'I think this is a great opportunity for you, and for the Army, as does Major Hudson. We are very happy for you. As long as you do have the leave, you may use it to attend Miss World.'

I stood there dumbfounded, barely able to open my mouth to thank him. Mercifully, he carried on talking.

'We've had a chat about the logistics, and we're trying to get someone in to replace you during your time away. You will have to come in tomorrow morning to talk him through the job. We will do a proper handover. We are now negotiating with Miss England to see if you can go a day or so later.'

It really takes something to shut me up, but this was unbelievable! They really were doing everything they could to make this happen. Only an hour ago I had assumed that I would ask permission out of politeness to Angie, but that my pageant ambitions were long forgotten. Now, it was dawning on me that I really was Miss England.

You might actually have to go through with this, I found myself thinking. It's the opportunity you always wanted, so you must seize it.

My colleagues were waiting breathlessly when I returned to my desk. I had only told a couple of them as Angie had been so specific that this could not reach the papers until things were confirmed, but the ones who knew were wriggling with excitement.

'So…?'

'I'm allowed to go. They're just sorting out final arrangements!'

'*Oh my God*!' was the general, barely contained, squeal throughout the office.

'I know!' I did a little jump up and down in my distinctly unglamorous Army uniform. 'I'm Miss England!'

When I got back to my desk I realised that my mobile almost had steam coming out of it, there were so many texts and voicemails from other Miss England girls and friends who knew I had come second. Anxiously, I went through them all. What was I supposed to say to people? It seemed the gossip-wheel was spinning wildly, and everyone wanted to chat about it but no one had considered that I might have been asked to replace Rachel at such short notice. For a moment, I ignored all the messages and started at my computer screen, trying to compose myself.

I only had twenty-four hours left at my desk for the next six weeks. How was I to get everything done on time? And how was I going to get myself ready for Miss World? Any five-week trip would be a major packing task but this one required non-stop glamour, several outfits a day, and weeks of preparation. I felt utterly overwhelmed. What had I said yes to?

I called Angie and she explained that she was going to start trying to organise the evening gowns, but that I would have to take the next afternoon off to buy everything else I'd need for the trip. Only an hour later Major Hudson confirmed that a replacement for me had been found and I would be able to leave work at lunchtime the next day.

That evening I went back to my room in the barracks and tried to think about what I needed to pack. I had to get myself sorted, but also I couldn't tell anyone apart from the small group of immediate colleagues that I was going. So I barricaded myself into my room, got down a suitcase from on top of the wardrobe and started laying out what I did – and didn't – need on the bed. In England, it was November, so I had barely anything for five weeks in South Africa. This would be one hell of a shopping trip.

While I was in my room, surrounded by half-written shopping lists and packing chaos, I heard a knock at the door.

'You coming down for dinner, Kat?' asked the girl from the room next door.

'Er, no, I'm watching...' I stabbed at the TV remote to see what was on. '...*EastEnders*.'

'Er... OK,' came the reply. She knew full well that I didn't really watch the programme. I couldn't have sounded more suspicious if I'd put on a fake French accent.

'Yeah, just having a quiet one,' I continued, desperately trying to sound innocent from the other side of the door. 'Catch you later!'

Anyone who knows me would have immediately understood that it was seriously strange for me to have missed a meal, but I couldn't take the risk of anyone coming in and spotting my semi-packed cases everywhere.

She would just have to be curious for the night. I went back to my shopping lists, only stopping when I saw a familiar name flash up on my mobile: Rachel Christie.

I answered, having no idea what conversation might follow.

'Hi Kat, it's Rachel.'

'Hi, how are you?'

'I've been better. You know how it is.'

'I'm so sorry about everything that's happened. I'm gutted for you,' I told her. I didn't dare to ask for any details – I knew Rachel and I had always really liked her, so I didn't want to go digging around, making her feel any worse than she probably already did.

'Yeah, me too.'

'Listen, have you spoken to Ang...?' (I wanted to find out if she knew what my plans were. It was going to be a massively awkward conversation if she didn't know that I was taking her place).

'Yes, yes, I have. That's why I was calling.'

'OK, I'm really sorry. I felt I had to say yes to Miss World, although obviously it's an amazing opportunity to carry on what I've been doing to promote the Army.'

'That's what I wanted to say. It *is* an amazing opportunity and I am just so sorry that it's happened this way for you. I have been planning for Miss World for months and I can't believe you're going to have to go so unprepared. If you were going to have to replace me, I would at least have wished that you could do it in a less stressful way.'

'Don't be silly, you don't have to apologise to me!'

'I feel like I do. It's such a mess. I can't think of anyone else I would have chosen to lose my crown to, and it's awful that you don't have any time to sort yourself out.'

'It's fine, it's fine – I just hope you're OK, too.'

'Listen, you can have any of my gowns. Most of them will fit you. Take whatever you need, Angie will sort it out. Just keep in touch and let me know how it all goes.'

'Of course, you take care too, though.'

With a heavy heart, I hung up. It was an awful, stilted conversation to have. I really felt for Rachel as I knew how much the title had meant to her and I had no way of fully expressing to her how excited I was, but how utterly panicked I really felt about the trip. At least we genuinely were friends, though: I don't think I could have gone if there had been a bad atmosphere with the girl I had taken over from, it would have been just too awkward. After all, I had forgotten all about Miss World until about twelve hours ago.

I put my careful heaps of packing on the floor and tried to get some sleep. Of course, the minute I closed my eyes all I could see were flying images of strappy sandals and false eyelashes and glamorous competitors. I barely slept a wink.

With morning came the news that although I was still going to be allowed to register late, I would have to be in London by 9am the next day. That helped me to realise that I really was Miss England – but it certainly didn't help with the tiny amount of time I had to get myself ready for the trip.

What happened that morning was amazing, though – really, I can't thank the Army enough. When I got to my desk, the lad who was taking over from me was there, ready for handover. The poor guy was so confused. From the atmosphere around me it was very obvious that I was going somewhere exciting, but I couldn't tell him where or why until it was officially announced. The security threat for the Army and the risk of it hitting the papers wasere too great, so I just had to explain everything in a whirlwind of attempted organisation.

'So, where are you off to?' he asked.

'Oh, never you mind!' I breezily replied at one point. By now, he seemed quite convinced that I was joining the SAS – and in a high-profile role at that. The office was tingly with excitement and all the while my phone was buzzing away as the messages piled in.

'Rachel *dethroned*!'

'Does this mean it's you? Are you Miss England?'

'What's going on re: Rachel? Any news?'

'Call me?'

'Call me!'

And several times over: 'CALL ME!!!'

In the end, I turned the phone on its face and ignored the lot. I wasn't about to start bragging until an official announcement had been made, nor could I face lying to anyone, so I had to avoid the situation entirely.

Just as the handover was wrapping up, a handful of in-the-know colleagues came creeping up to my desk, huge grins plastered across their faces. From behind one of their backs came a bottle of champagne, followed by a few plastic cups from the kitchen. They had got me a card, done a whip-round and everyone had signed it. All of that organising in such a short space of time, I couldn't believe it. As I thanked them all, my heart was in my mouth: I realised my true value to the team and was so glad that I had been working so hard for the last few months to get such a respectful (and fun!) send-off. Suddenly the office was a blur of clinking glasses, hugs and congratulations. Watching this spectacle was my temporary replacement, now more confused than ever. By this stage, I was pretty sure he was convinced that I was starting work as a top-level spy!

If my replacement had seen me drive out of the barracks that day, he would have been even convinced. I really was on a mission, it's just that it wasn't to be a secret agent mission: this was a shopping mission. It was early afternoon by the time I left the barracks in Frimley. The night before, I had found out that the nearest shopping centre with late-night facilities was in Basingstoke, somewhere I'd never been before. I managed to persuade a friend to take the afternoon off work and swooped by to pick her up. As she got into the passenger seat, we grinned at each other, then gave a high five.

'We are going SHOPPING!' I whooped.

COMBAT TO CATWALK

I was sick with nerves, but the afternoon that followed was one of the most bizarre and exciting I have ever had. Angie had transferred £5,000 of the Miss England budget to get what I needed and it had just arrived in my account. What followed was the shopping trip of a lifetime.

This is what was on my shopping list:

- Five weeks' worth of toiletries, fake tan, eyelashes, hair products, make-up, scent
- Five weeks' worth of sportswear – enough to have a different outfit for each day's sports round, as well as clothes for rehearsals
- Five weeks' worth of suits and formal wear for the daily interviews
- Five weeks' worth of daywear, for meal times and daytimes when we weren't doing specific activities
- Five weeks' worth of evening gowns
- Five weeks' worth of shoes to go with each of these outfits.

At Miss World, I would be expected to do my own hair and make-up every day for five weeks, and I would need a wardrobe that could stand up to those of girls who had been preparing and budgeting for weeks and months on end. The culture of Miss World is that you are being judged twenty-four hours a day; you cannot let standards slip, and you can't be seen in the same thing twice. At Miss World, 'casual' merely means 'not a ball gown'. To prepare for an event like that, I would have bought a new notebook and spent hours poring over the perfect lists, comparing prices on the Internet and finding the most travel-friendly cosmetics packaging, but now all I had were some scribbled notes from the night before and a very patient friend. By the time we parked up, we had a plan, though.

When we arrived at Debenhams my pal headed straight for the luggage department and got two of the biggest suitcases she could find, which she immediately wheeled over to me. Meanwhile, I was at the Christian Dior counter, which I had approached with an enormous smile.

'Hi there, do you work on commission?'

'Yes, I do,' replied the girl behind the counter. I don't look like an especially wealthy person and I was scruffy with stress, wearing tracksuit bottoms. She must have thought I was wildly patronising, about to spend thirty quid on a bottle of scent. Instead, I spent £600 in 20 minutes: lip-gloss, mascara, eyeliner, blusher, powder, primer, and two bottles of scent... the LOT! The girl serving me could not believe her eyes. Just as I was finishing, the suitcases turned up. I shoved the carrier bags into one of them and we wheeled them over to the shoe department. As luck would have it, there was a sale on. Once again, I approached the assistant, grinning.

'Excuse me, could you show me what you have in a size five?'

'Yes, of course – it's this rack here.'

'Thank you, I'll take the lot.'

The assistant did a huge double take.

'You'll *what?*'

'I'll take the lot, please. No duplicates, please – one of each. I don't have time to try them on.'

She must have thought I had lost the plot entirely but I really didn't have time to try anything on. I could see there was one gold pair, one silver, a couple of black pairs and a few colours – that would have to do. A few minutes later, we were shoving the 15 pairs I'd just bought into one of the suitcases.

Next, we wheeled our way to the sportswear section. A pattern was developing...

'Excuse me, please could you show me what you have in a size 8–10?'

'Yes, of course – it's over here.'

'I'll take it.'

'Take *what?*'

'All of it.'

'Excuse me?'

'I need 35 separate outfits. Is that a problem?'

'No, of course not: I'll just pop to the stockroom for you.'

I made sure I got a couple of pairs of box-fresh trainers, performed the same procedure with the formal suits and shoved it all into a suitcase with the rest of my haul. Luckily, Angie called in the interim to let me know that she was on the case with the gowns.

By this time, people were starting to point and whisper. Who is she? Where is she going? Why is she shopping like that? After all, it was just Basingstoke on a Friday afternoon. Small children were starting to look bewildered as I strolled by with my suitcases of booty.

Later that evening I found out that someone in the UK had won the Euromillions lottery; I imagine anyone in Debenhams that day may have suspected that person was me. All I knew was that I couldn't tell anyone the truth until the official announcement had been made, so I had to stagger on anonymously.

Next, we had to hit Boots for essentials: we filled six baskets in 40 minutes. Then came what I suspect might be my greatest achievement as Miss England: I managed to spend £700 in Primark! To this day, I don't even know how that's possible. I knew I needed a lot of different brightly-coloured summer clothes, and finding that kind of thing on a November evening in Surrey is not especially easy. I wasn't thrilled by the prospect of wearing high-street clothes to Miss World, but hey, I was just pleased to be going and happy to have found some lighter things.

Eventually, we had done all we could. My pal threw the suitcases in the back of the car and forced me to a nearby bar to have a celebratory cocktail. I was starting to spiral into a giddy frenzy of packing and panic, when really all I needed was to just sit down and process everything that was going on. As our glasses clinked, I suddenly felt overwhelmed at the realisation that I wasn't even going to be able to see my other friends or my family before heading off to Miss World; I wouldn't get to see anyone until

Christmas and some might be after that. Obviously I had survived my time in Iraq without too much homesickness but then I had known when I was going, I'd said some proper goodbyes and been properly prepared. However, I was equally thrilled that I was heading off to somewhere so totally different this time: it was Miss World, for heaven's sake! I was still tingly with excitement from the afternoon's shopping and festivities but the idea of no proper goodbyes momentarily cast a little shadow of sadness over it all.

When I was back in my room I sat down on the bed and immediately called everyone I trusted to tell them my news. I was at once cheered when I heard my mum's voice and she told me how thrilled they all were for me; she also reminded me that the five weeks would whizz by and I really should not be wishing the time away. She was – as mums always are – quite right. I surveyed the room, with Army boots and combats in one corner and a monster pile of false eyelashes in another, and realised I had some serious organisation to do.

Packing seemed an impossible task as I didn't know what dresses Angie would have sorted out for me: if you ever imagine yourself at Miss World, you always have a clear image of yourself in 'That Dress', the one you wear to the final, the one where you look like the very best you can be. That was how my red Miss England dress had made me feel and I'd always imagined that if I made it to Miss World, I'd have something even more spectacular. But this time, I had no idea what I'd be wearing for the final: at this stage, I had no evening dresses at all! Life's too short, I eventually thought to myself. I took all unnecessary packaging off everything I'd bought in the two suitcases and then devoted myself to trying to get a bit of sleep.

Just as I felt myself dropping off, I remembered something else: I had had no tan, no nails and no hair done. I staggered out of bed and left a message at my hairdressers, begging to see if I could come in first thing for a blow-dry, if nothing else. I woke to a text confirming my appointment: OK, I would be pale and my hair might need a trim, but I was going to register for Miss World with decent hair somehow!

As soon as my hair was done, I drove up to London with my mum. Meanwhile, my mobile was tweeting away for the entire drive as the press had now been informed that there was a new Miss England: Kat Hodge. On the motorway, we stopped at a petrol station and grabbed a selection of newspapers, quickly flicking through them to check the coverage before continuing the journey. Mum drove while I read bits out to her, in between calling my friends back. The papers seemed pretty positive about me, but I definitely got the sense that now they had a whiff of scandal, they'd be hungry for more. On the other hand, my friends were ecstatic. One of the most satisfying moments of the whole experience came when I changed my Facebook status to 'Kat Hodge is… MISS ENGLAND' and immediately had another wave of calls.

Angie had arranged for me to meet her at the Hilton Hotel where the Miss England finals had been held so that we could sort out final preparations and I could steady my nerves. Also, I needed to try on some of the evening dresses that she had brought with her. As I walked back through the big gold doors of the hotel, I felt choked with tears: a few months ago I had left it as an exhausted runner-up, now I was returning as Miss England. I was equally exhausted, but Miss England nonetheless!

But the sight that I saw when I entered the hotel room helped to convince me of my title: Angie was sitting there, perched on the dressing-table chair, and standing next to her was the dress designer Karen Karmody. Draped over the entire bed and every other space in the room were several stunning, glittering gowns. Karen is an incredible designer and she had created Rachel's dress for the Miss England final; Rachel was a similar size to me and so the plan was for me to try on as many of her gowns as possible to see if I could fit into them with a few alterations.

The first dress I tried was the one that had been made for the Miss World final. It was white, a column dress with a train, covered from head to foot in tiny crystals and utterly stunning, like something a princess would wear. But I am a pale girl with dark hair, so I worried that it washed me out a bit: I felt a little sad that circumstances meant I was going to be wearing a dress that really didn't suit me.

All was not lost, though as one of the other dresses that Karen had brought was an absolute knockout. It was red, my colour, and covered in tiny sparkles. When I tried it on, I immediately felt 'me' and Angie and Karen could tell. We decided this would be the dress that I would wear there and then to have a couple of publicity photographs taken for Miss England.

Before long, a photographer and his assistant were up in the room and once I had changed and made up, they got out a Miss England background screen and started snapping away. It felt so weird: I was there in my gown, wearing my crown and my sash for the first time! But instead of having been presented with them in front of a cheering crowd, I was in a little hotel room and Angie had got the crown out of a box filled with bubble wrap. No one else had seen me as Miss England: there had been no ceremony, no public fuss yet. There was still a tiny part of me that felt as if it wasn't happening. However, all that changed when we arrived by cab at the Grosvenor House Hotel on Park Lane. I was unloading the cases with Angie when a Miss World representative stepped out of the opulent entrance and came towards us, saying: 'Aha, Miss England! Welcome, we have been looking forward to meeting you.'

It was the first time that I had been addressed by my official title: it did have happy-making sound. As I walked into the reception area, my confidence was boosted and I held my head high.

The formalities of registering were over pretty quickly, and Angie was there with me, but the next stage was two photo calls to commemorate the opening of Miss World 2009. As I entered the room one of the organisers casually informed me that several members of the press were there just for me but I didn't know whether or not to take them seriously. All the other girls seemed so gorgeous, so poised, while I was there in my last-minute dress and my half-packed bags; it seemed unlikely that I would hold their attention. After all, there were about 60 of us girls entering the room and I have never in my life been to a place filled with so many beautiful women. They were every colour, every shape and every style but each and every one of them was an absolute drop-dead beauty. I could barely stop staring: I was so mesmerised by the overwhelming glamour, the buzz of international chattering and the excited atmosphere among us all.

Well, they probably won't even be able to identify me from among all the other stunners, I told myself, as I took a deep breath and strode into the room. But I had forgotten one key fact: we were all in our evening gowns, complete with crowns and sashes. If you're wearing a big sash that says 'MISS ENGLAND', it is of course pretty easy for any photographer to identify you. And it didn't take long: within minutes, I could hear the men shouting at me.

'Kat!'

'Over here!'

'Kat!'

'Miss England!'

'Could you step out so we can get you alone!'

'Katherine!'

'Give us a smile!'

'Katrina!'

'Over here, newbie!'

The press were becoming more and more intense: in fact, they were bordering on rude. Just as in the first-ever shoot that I did with the Miss England bikinis, I found myself blinking into their camera flashes, barely knowing where to look. For about forty minutes I stood there, dazzled, trying to smile politely and deflect some of the attention back to the other girls. Eventually an official decided enough was enough and announced that it was time for the 'Team UK and Ireland' press call.

This one was for me, Miss Ireland, Miss Northern Ireland, Miss Scotland and Miss Wales. I had never met any of the girls before, but clearly they had already had time to bond with each other. Of course they all had a language in common, but it was more than that: they formed a wall of blonde perfection. I took one look at them and wanted to yelp with anxiety, 'But you're all perfect! And *so* blonde – I am *so* the odd one out here!'

Luckily, the girls knew who I was and why I was so late to the event. Quickly, they quickly formed a protective circle of support around me that lasted almost for the rest of the competition. I would have been lost without them.

After that final photo call, which was no less stressful than the original one, I headed up to my room, where I realised that I was going to be roommates with Miss

Ireland, aka Laura, for the whole trip. And I could not have wished for a better room buddy: despite her intimidating blonde perfection, she was the most smiley, loveliest girl, a real credit to her home. The minute she came in and saw me staring at my suitcases, trying to work out what else I needed to pack, she insisted we go through her clothes too and work out what I could borrow.

'We can double up!' she explained. 'Anything you want to borrow, anything you might have forgotten, just tell me. I practically have two of everything, anyway.'

I will confirm: she did have a lot of stuff, but I was so touched by her immediate willingness to share and to lend. After all, we were meant to be competitors.

The next morning, I had to be up early to attend an extra event in the Miss World schedule: an international press conference for me and me alone, to mark my introduction to Miss England. Facing the press pack was overwhelming, to say the least: I knew I had the personality to deal politely with reporters who were excited by the scent of a Miss England scandal, but it was still a delicate process. There were two key things that they wanted to talk about, but I really couldn't discuss either of them in any detail. There was no way that I was going to compromise the security of my colleagues in Iraq or Afghanistan by going into details of my time serving abroad, nor did I know enough about the situation with Rachel Christie's arrest to offer up any salacious comments. She is my friend, so I was never going to say anything cruel about her. And she was still on bail, so I was keen not to get involved in the legal issues. The questions were relentless, though – they kept asking away, doing their best to trip me up and get me to say something mean or rude. One journalist seemed to be trying to imply that I was gay because I didn't want to talk about my personal life, while another was asking if I had abandoned a trip to Afghanistan to parade around in frocks; almost all of them wanted me to say with relish that I thought Rachel was guilty of assault and should have been dethroned.

Somehow I managed to keep my nerve and after several hours of interviews, one of the Miss World staff finally suggested it was time to go. Eventually I went up to my hotel room to pack and check if there was anything else that I needed Angie to sort out for me. Minutes later, Laura came in and flopped down onto the bed.

'What are you doing in the talent round?' she asked casually.

I hadn't even remembered there was one.

'Umm?' was the only reply I could think of. There was no way that I would get permission to do my usual Army routine as a talent, no time to ask for permission to take my uniform out of the country or wear it in the competition and the idea of taking a weapon for the rifle drill as I had done in my Miss England DVD was out of the question. Usually I had fallen back on the individuality and strength that my Army role gave me whenever I felt nervous in a pageant situation: this time, with the competition being abroad, I couldn't rely on it. But I quickly told myself that facing the talent round unprepared was always going to be one step down from taking on an armed Iraqi unprepared, so there was no need to get myself into a state. Instead, I would have to rely on good old-fashioned instinct and confidence, so I grabbed my phone and texted Angie.

'Can you get me a Shirley Bassey backing track? I've just remembered the talent round,' I asked.

'Can you sing?' came the reply.

'I'm going to have to,' was my answer.

I sat on my bed and put my head in my hands. How could I have forgotten such a key part of the competition? I felt as if I was never going to get on top of things: I had yet to finish packing properly, none of my evening gowns had arrived from having their alterations done by Karen Karmody, I was meant to be leaving in a few minutes to go on a sightseeing trip around London with the other contestants, and now I had to worry about backing tracks as well. Just when I least wanted to, I burst into tears. Laura immediately tried to calm me down and told me that everything would be OK in the end, but it was all just too much for me.

Moments later, Angie called back about the music and she could immediately tell that I was trying to stop myself from crying.

'Wait there, I'll call back in five minutes,' she told me.

When my phone rang again, she said that I no longer had to go on the sightseeing trip. Miss World had agreed that as I had clearly seen England before and as I had so much to catch up on, I could spend the afternoon having a rest and getting myself sorted.

When Laura returned from the trip and gave me a huge hug, I realised it wasn't the glamour that was the reason why I was a Miss World contestant after all, it was my personality. I had proved that I was a strong, ambitious girl who had something to say for herself so the last thing I should be doing was sitting in my room, sobbing over sequins; I had served in Iraq, and that was part of the reason why I was there. Time to start behaving like the girl I had told them all that I was.

So I took a few deep breaths, put on an evening dress and headed downstairs with the others for the Miss World opening gala.

CHAPTER NINE

MISS WORLD

THE MISS World opening gala, on 9 November 2009, was all I had imagined it would be, and more. In truth, it left me feeling rather overwhelmed by the glitz, glamour and above all, the sheer number of us competitors there. Looking around the room at any given time, it seemed completely impossible that I would ever be able to remember any of the girls' names, let alone be a realistic competitor.

I managed to get a good night's sleep, though as the next morning the competition officially began. And once you are taking part in Miss World, you are taking part in it all the time: from the moment you wake up to the time when you close your hotel bedroom door at night, the judges are keeping an eye on you. Not only do you need to be looking your absolute best at all times, whether it's as you pour the cream in your morning coffee or carry your bags across the airport, but you need to behave in a suitable way, too.

As a result, I headed down to breakfast with my nerves all a-jangle, trying to remind myself that I had faced considerably bigger and more dangerous challenges in life. What would my Army colleagues think if they knew last-minute nervousness was nipping away at my ankles again? But my nerves were brushed aside once more by the fact that we were to be given a talk by Julia Morley, the president of Miss World, that morning.

If there is anyone out there interested in the pageant world who doesn't know Julia, shame on you: she is a part of its creation! Julia's husband was Eric Morley, the creator of *Come Dancing* (which inspired *Strictly Come Dancing*), the Mecca Bingo empire and of course, Miss World and Miss England; she is a legend in the world of glitz and glamour. She is definitelymay be an older woman now, but I don't think she will fully retire until the entire world is covered in sequins – her whole career has been based on bringing more glamour and sparkle to the world.

When comedians or journalists refer to the cliché of Miss World contestants saying they dream of 'world peace', that is Julia Morley's doing: she really, truly *does* want to bring about world peace by getting nations together in these international pageants. Every year, she helps to raise millions of pounds for charity and has probably raised billions in her lifetime. Julia is just the kind of person who I imagine has Shirley Bassey's number on speed dial and can call her up for a chat about floor-length gowns, should the mood take her.

But she is much more than that: she genuinely cares about all of the girls taking part in the competitions and she wants to see them achieve their best. What's more, she has a warm, honest heart and has never been anything other than sweet natured to us all. She is very softly spoken, with a slightly shaky voice now, so when she talks to you, you find yourself leaning in to give her your undivided attention. She's the mother hen of Miss World, which makes you want to never let her down.

That morning over breakfast Julia arrived to give us a little talk and to wish us luck for the coming weeks. My anxieties were eased enormously helped when she addressed us, saying that we should not try and compare ourselves to the other girls nor be jealous or judgmental about what they had. Different nations have different budgets and different sponsorship for their Miss World entrants. Miss South Africa is as famous as Angelina Jolie in her country, whereas other countries are not at all interested in their entrant. We were encouraged to take pride in ourselves, as we were all winners already – after all, we were representing our countries and we deserved to wear that with confidence.

Then she told us a story from a few years ago that really struck me, about Miss Iceland: she was an absolutely beautiful girl, but she had very little money. She had worn the same hot pants and a vest top in most of the events for six weeks and even had to customise her mother's wedding dress to make do as her ball gown in the glamour round. But she was talented, charismatic and well liked by everyone. And she went on to win Miss World that year as simply because she'd had the right attitude. I realised then how much I had to offer: there was hope for me yet!

That's what Miss World is all about: it's a competition that has a reputation for being after the girl with the shiniest white teeth and no doubt Julia Morley loves it, but she looks for much more than that – she looks for a bit of spirit in a girl.

What followed after breakfast were two of my biggest challenges yet of the entire Miss World experience: phoning all of my loved ones to say goodbye (it took forever!) and sitting on my suitcases to finally get them to shut. After all the shopping Angie had done and the enormous box of dresses from Karen Karmody, it was quite a task. Then, finally, we were off to the airport. I honestly believe that I might have gone mad if I'd had any more time to prepare and fret – my whirlwind of getting ready in record time was probably the best thing that could have happened to me.

When I arrived at Heathrow with all the other girls, there had been so much press coverage of my sudden coronation as Miss England that the airport staff recognised me and rushed me through check-in with full

VIP treatment. It felt intensely weird to be recognised on such a wide level, but what a way to say goodbye to the country you are off to represent. Abu Dhabi, here I come!

Because of my experiences in the Army – having to grab sleep when you can, regardless of whether you're wearing smelly uniform, in a freezing-cold truck in the rain or in a hot and sticky tent in the desert – I'm very good at sneaking in a kip wherever possible. This meant that I slept for most of the flight to Abu Dhabi and was able to fully take in the mind-blowing opulence of the Yas Hotel when I got there. Built in the centre of the country's Formula One track, it's a temple of sleek modern design. If I had been any more tired, I think I might have suspected I was hallucinating again as not long after checking in, we were whisked off to lunch at the Emirates Palace Hotel, the most expensive hotel in the world. Made mostly of gold and fit not just for a king but an entire royal family, it was a once-in-a-lifetime venue.

After a few days, several dress fittings and a couple of gold-inspired catwalk shows, we left Abu Dhabi for the competition's main destination: South Africa. It was a night flight, which meant I could easily have had a really good sleep on the plane, but on this occasion I found myself watching the in-flight movie: *My Sister's Keeper*. Instead of getting all the beauty sleep that I could, in a moment of complete madness I became utterly gripped and found myself sobbing all the way through! This would have been fine – a little sleep missed, but no major harm done – except for the fact that the South Africans had laid on such a splendid welcome for us at the airport. I was completely taken aback and looking a bit of a state, with hastily wiped mascara streaks on my face, when drummers, dancers, singers and the nation's press all appeared at the Arrivals lounge, all at 4am local time! It was not my finest hour, but buzzing with excitement to be in Johannesburg, I chalked it up to experience and got on with the competition.

After all the excitement of the travel, the dresses and the sights, I had almost forgotten that I was actually taking part in a competition – and one that I had barely prepared for. After lunch on our first day in South Africa, we were off to rehearsals for the talent round. I was longing to be totally 'Miss Congeniality' about it and start up on my Army displays, but with no time to prepare either a display or sort out the legalities of doing it abroad, I was left with singing as my talent. Suddenly, those days at the BRIT School felt like a very long time ago! Unfortunately, I'm not blessed with a voice to rival Leona Lewis's and after the flights I had picked up a bit of an infection and had a dreadful sore throat, which meant that I could hardly speak, let alone sing, but the organisers seemed to appreciate the situation I was in and went pretty easy on me.

Later in the week I was given the opportunity for a one-on-one singing session with Mike Dixon, a top producer who has even worked with Shirley Bassey. By then, my sore throat was clearing up and I was just about able to get to the end of 'Big Spender' without sounding too much like Lily Savage. However, Mike decided on 'All That Jazz' from the musical *Chicago* as the one for me. It wasn't exactly a showstopper, but it was the best I had and I wasn't going to let it get in the way of me enjoying my moment on the stage or doing my best for England. Poor old Laura, with whom I was still sharing, was probably becoming thoroughly sick of my constant warm-up exercises and rehearsals in the room!

In between rehearsals for the various rounds and the show itself, we continued to have an incredible and hugely privileged time exploring everything that South Africa has to offer. One day I would be wearing a stunning gold Karen Karmody dress to attend a dinner in honour of key South African charities and the next we'd be visiting a Penguin hospital on the coast! Much as I adored the sensational dresses that I was lucky enough to wear (and the gold one was a real belter!), it was some of the nature that we got to see that really took my breath away. Watching the King African Penguins – now an endangered species – up close was an extraordinary moment. We were supposed to be helping to release some of the rescued and healed penguins back into the wild, but the weather was dreadfully windy that day and so we weren't able to do so, but it was still felt like a story to tell the grandchildren one day.

A week or two later, we were also taken on safari.

Laura and I, who were by now firm friends, thought that as we'd be outside in the back of a jeep all day we wouldn't need to look 100 per cent glammed up. How wrong could we have been! When we emerged from our room, with hair in neat tied-back plait pigtails and the bare minimum of make-up, we were taken aback to see that everyone else there was still sticking to the huge curls, long lashes and big talons that had characterised every other day so far.

I stand by our decision, though, as we had so much fun in those safari vehicles, with the wind hitting us as we drove around, looking out over the top at all sorts of animals. But we had only been out for an hour or two before we heard an enormous crack of thunder, the sky turned charcoal as if someone had just drawn the curtains, and the heavens opened. Our safari guide asked if we wanted to carry on, and enticed by the idea of seeing lions and cheetahs, we said that of course we did. Laura and I were more than glad to be in simple hair and make-up as the downpour hit us.

Before long, however, the rain had cleared up and we were able to dispense with our delightful plastic ponchos. Soon after that, we were given the chance to hold baby lions and get up close to a family of cheetahs. Yes, I have served in the Army and faced very real danger before, but I must admit much as I wanted to connect with such a clever animal in the wild and feel the unbelievable softness of his coat, I was genuinely terrified when I touched a lion for the very first time. Just as I was getting my nerve up, one of them leapt out of his resting position and bounded towards a photographer. Were we toast? No, it seemed he fancied a bit of a leg stretch rather than a snack, but the shot of adrenaline I felt was up there with my most intense moments in Iraq!

We travelled all over South Africa and spending so much time with all the other girls meant that we really got to know each other and to learn about each other's countries and their approaches to beauty and women in society. We were like an enormous travelling boarding school, attended by some of the most beautiful – and giggly – girls in the world. I really enjoyed the sense of camaraderie that developed between us all with each passing week. The majority of the girls spoke English as a second language, if at all, but luckily I spoke enough Spanish to have chats with more of the girls than some others were able to. Speaking slowly and politely for over a month is no mean feat, but it was really worth it to hear so many different perspectives on life – and of course, so many beauty tips!

I adored Laura, of course, and by the end of the five and half weeks we were practically sisters, but I also made close friendships with Miss Wales (Lucy), Miss Northern Ireland (Cherie) and Miss Sierra Leone (Mariatu), who was the craziest, most high-spirited girl you could ever imagine meeting. Always smiling, always good for a laugh and happy to share make-up tips and accessories, she was exactly the kind of person I would never have even come across, let alone have the chance to become friends with, if not for Miss World. She had travelled to China for six months to learn how to eat fire and do a face-change act – where she changed masks without you noticing – for the talent round; it was astonishing.

Meanwhile, Miss USA was nothing like you might have imagined: there wasn't a whiff of hairspray following her around, but instead she was a super-cool surf girl from Malibu, who was definitely happiest in the kind of beachwear that she grew up in. Similarly, Miss Australia was a bit of a swearing, ballsy girl who didn't suffer fools gladly. We were quite a bunch!

I didn't want to forget anyone and so one day when we visited a local market, I bought a notebook and decided to ask all of the 113 girls to sign it so that I would remember each of them – and know how to say a few words in each of their languages when I got home. By then, this time would probably all seem like a dream. I wanted to make sure that I remembered we didn't just sit around all day talking about our dreams of world peace: we were the modern face of Miss World and didn't want anyone telling us otherwise!

There were some low times too, of course: I missed home a lot and every now and then, I would go to an event, take a look around me at the other girls and find myself thinking, what am I doing here? How have I got myself involved with this? Why am I wasting my time – and everyone else's – when the competition is so gorgeous and talented?

But if I ever spoke to any of the other girls about it then I would soon realise that everyone there was having moments like that too, and we were better off sharing and sticking together than taking it out on each other. Not being able to have a day off from 100 per cent glamour is exhausting to say the least and once or twice, I had to remind myself how much I had wanted to go there.

Every now and again Laura and myself, and perhaps a couple of the other girls, would find ourselves sneaking off to our rooms to snack on a few biscuits and take an hour or two off from being perfect. I would love to say there was more naughtiness and scandal that I found out about on the trip, but in all honesty everyone seemed to be very respectful and hardworking throughout. Maybe it was the huge amount of security that we had around us most of the time, perhaps it was due to the fact that Julia Morley herself turned up for so many of the events, or it was just that we had too much respect for the organisation, but I'm afraid scandal was thin on the ground.

There were also a few mornings when we'd wake up, see all of the girly paraphernalia that is part and parcel of looking the part every day, know that all of the rooms around us were even worse and sigh a deep sigh.

'Five minute make-up job today?' one of us would say to the other and we would race each other to get ready as fast as possible. Because Laura's blonde and I'm brunette, we were able to double up with clothes and accessories so it didn't matter that I was somewhat lacking in clothes. We truly did live the Julia Morley dream of bringing countries together... through the power of accessories! Some days you just didn't want to wear five different cocktail dresses in a day, so switching certain details on the outfits served us well.

Laura and I certainly needed each other – and the sense of humour that we developed between us – as there were a few times when someone with a whisker less confidence might have been totally thrown by the situation. And the day I went to collect my golden bikini for the swimsuit round was one of them.

The theme for the entire competition that year was 'gold' so instead of the traditional red or white bikinis, we were in gold for the swimwear round. I was already pretty confident that this wasn't going to be a round that I would excel in, but when we were given our outfits I realised I truly didn't have a chance: I had been given a bikini made to Rachel Christie's measurements! It was like a thong. Those bikinis would have been pretty small on me, anyway – they were not what you might call matronly – but this was something else. There was no way I could have worn it without causing an embarrassing scandal. I tried it on in front of Laura to see if she thought I was overreacting. Her response was a delicate: 'Oh deeeeeaaaaar!'

As there was nothing else for me to wear that would not have entirely undermined the look of the competition, I was allowed to sit out that section while they were judging and making the videos to show. It was a huge relief. I always feel a bit silly pouting at the camera and this is something that more of the girls do in the bikini round. To me, it's more natural to smile as in my opinion there is a huge difference between a broad smile from a confident, attractive girl who is interested in expressing herself in a stylish way, making the very best of both her figure and her personality and a girl pulling a 'sexy face'. I believe the former is considerably more attractive than the latter and I think most men would agree with me, too.

The vast majority of the girls were so keen to proudly represent their country, but as ever there were one or two who looked as if deep down, they had their eye on the potentially more lucrative goal of something like *Playboy*. But that path is not for me, as I can't think of anything less of a turn-on than someone really trying to be sexy.

Another close shave, fashion-wise, was when we all went down to Cape Town for the football World Cup draw. We were taking part in a huge photo shoot to promote the World Cup and once again, supplied with entirely gold outfits. Yes, *entirely* gold – gold T-shirts, gold trainers, gold peaked caps and gold hot pants! Wearing that outfit, it would be hard not to look like the Jules Rimet trophy itself. But then at the last minute, we were told that if we were from a nation who had qualified for the World Cup, we could wear the football strip for that country. I did a

massive whoop when we were told. Thank you, England –
you're my lads!

Even better, a secondary part of the trip was to be a
photo shoot with David Beckham as part of England's
campaign for the 2018 World Cup bid. I was beside
myself with excitement and had told all my friends and
family back in England. It was without doubt the bit of
my trip that they were most jealous of, no matter what I
told them about holding lions and staying in billionaire
hotels!

Arriving at the shoot, David Beckham was already there,
sitting in a corner and quietly eating a chicken Caesar
salad. I played it cool and just smiled politely at him when
I saw him, but then a few minutes later he didn't seem to
be there any more. Later, I found out that he had just been
informed that his grandfather had died and had
immediately left. I don't blame him – his grandfather is
known to have been such a huge supporter of his football
and I know I would have been devastated if it had been me.

Beckham aside, the magical experiences continued. We
planted trees in restored parks, went to the South African
President Jacob Zuma's house and met the man himself
and then we visited Nelson Mandela's house in Soweto,
which was a great privilege that I'll never forget.

In between all of this, I continued to fit in a lot of press.
I was whisked off to give interviews to Australian
breakfast TV (where I found I had lots of fans), I was still
doing press for journalists in the UK and it seemed the

South African press had taken quite a shine to me, too. The more press I got, the more people didn't seem to be able to believe that I really was in the Army: I did feel a bit naked without that part of my identity as I had always enjoyed promoting that side of my life and career before. In the end, I managed to convince everyone that I was for real, though!

Finally, after weeks of rehearsal – which were pretty complicated with 113 girls and several interpreters trying to convey what the next dance steps would be to them all – the big night finally came around on 12 December 2009. It was the show that we had all been working towards, being transmitted to two billion viewers worldwide for three hours. Internationally, it is the second most popular TV show of all time, beaten only by the World Cup.

Going out on stage at Miss World is like nothing you can ever imagine: as a young girl, I used to watch the competition in awe and I still felt shocked that this time I was actually a part of it. The stage and auditorium are so enormous that you can't even focus far back enough to see the end of the audience. The lights, the set, the dresses... it's beyond dazzling.

The show began with children holding all the nations' flags running out onto the stage and then we were introduced individually. I felt a huge rush of pride as they called out Miss England and when the camera zoomed in, I knew the time that I had spent trying to practise a 'perfect' smile in the mirror had been entirely wasted – I couldn't help but beam a huge, natural smile! Sometimes excitement and pride just cannot be contained.

By then, I knew that I had not done well enough in the talent and bikini rounds, so I was pretty sure when I walked on stage that I would not walk off as Miss World. But it was such an extraordinary event to be a part of that I just wanted to soak up each and every moment of it, so that I would be able to tell my children and grandchildren about it in years to come. Just making it there felt like a bonus and I was still half expecting someone to tap me on the shoulder to say there had been a horrible mistake.

The evening seemed to fly by, including the section when we were out there in our national costume, which saw me in a Victorian outfit of full skirt and corset, looking not unlike Jane Eyre! Before I knew it, they were announcing the top fifteen in the competition. I didn't make it, but some of the girls who had become close friends were in the top seven. I stood on stage with my fingers crossed for Miss France, Miss South Africa, Miss Gibraltar and Miss Colombia.

Tension rose throughout the area as the standard had been so high that it really could have been any of them – they weren't just stunningly beautiful girls, but engaging women, who had been a delight to be around for the entire competition and had excelled in the talent round as well. I really, really wanted it to be Miss Gibraltar, a natural beauty called Kaiane, but it was a nail-biting finish.

First of all the host announced that the third place had

gone to Miss South Africa. The home crowd went wild! Then, second place was Miss Mexico – a second roar of excitement. And finally…it was announced that the winner was Miss Gibraltar. I was thrilled! This was a huge achievement for Gibraltar as the country had never even been placed in the top fifteen in the 50 years that they had been taking part in the competition, let alone won it. And it was a wonderful accolade for Kaiane, who was without doubt one of the nicest girls there and a truly natural beauty. I was overjoyed for her personally, but I also felt that it was a great decision as it showed to girls all over the world that all the dull plastic beauty that is celebrated in so many other places wasn't welcome there. Kaiane is a fantastic role model, someone who young girls can look up to without feeling there is no hope that they could achieve their dreams, too.

You never think that you're going to be able to say that you are mates with Miss World, but now I really was! At the after-party that night we all let our hair down and celebrated properly. I had my photograph taken with Kaiane and also met her parents, who were beaming with pride and barely knew what to say to anyone, they were so overwhelmed by the experience.

As I got into bed that night, I knew that my Miss World adventures were now coming to an end. It had been the best experience of my life – the travel, the opportunities, the history, the wildlife and above all, the people. Part of me was happy to know that I wouldn't have to put on any make-up for a good long time, but another part just wanted to know what was coming next in my life. As I stared out of the plane window while it taxied along the runway the next morning, I felt excited about Christmas and seeing my friends and family again, but I also wondering whether or not the Army was going to agree to my career break to allow me act as Miss England.

While I was away, I put the wheels in motion for taking some formal, unpaid leave from the Army in order to perform my Miss England duties to the best of my ability. A once-in-a-lifetime experience, I wanted to give my full attention to it, to raise as much awareness and money as I possibly could for the Forces' charities and causes that mean so much to me. I was also conscious that staying at work throughout the time as Miss England might distract my colleagues, which wouldn't be fair. And I also had to bear in mind that I could not guarantee that I would not be given a posting abroad. If there's one thing that Miss England really needed, it's to be in England!

Plans were not finalised by the time I arrived home, however. I landed at the airport and the next day I was in my combats again. It was very strange, but I can't deny that they're more comfortable than heels and a ball gown! It was a small consolation when my car broke down on the side of the M25 that morning, though: only 48 hours before I had been preparing to face a worldwide audience among the most beautiful women in the world and now I was standing in the icy rain – shivering, and wondering if I'd get in trouble for turning up late for work. Yes, Miss England was back on home turf, with all that that entailed!

CHAPTER TEN

MY AMAZING YEAR

I SPENT CHRISTMAS and New Year as both a serving soldier and Miss England, but finally, on 12 January 2010, it was confirmed that I had been given a career break from the Army to fulfil my duties as Miss England. The weird thing was, the snow that had enveloped the entire country made it feel as if there was barely an England to be the 'Miss' of: everyone was snowed in, it seemed, with trains at a standstill and events cancelled, up and down the country. It was a bizarre way to start my duties, as it felt like a lot of waiting around to begin with; even my crowning party was postponed and wasn't held until the end of January.

After two years' worth of competitions, the accolade I had never thought would be awarded was finally mine. The event was held at Guildford Manor Hall and was a glitzy affair for press, Miss England competitors and those friends and family who could make it through the snow. As the occasion began, I walked down a long aisle towards the Miss England throne, which was at the front of the stage: it really was as if I was going to a coronation. Some music was playing and then Angie, the director of Miss England, read out a tribute to me while a singer performed 'Hallelujah'. Laura Coleman took the Miss England crown from her head and placed it on mine. At that moment I felt as if someone was about to wake me up and tell me to get back to normal life; things like this don't really happen to girls like me! But I had already proved they can.

The moment I was wearing the crown for the first time I had the biggest smile on my face that you could possibly imagine; it felt like it belonged. And the best bit is, no matter how many times I lend the crown to my mates, I'm the only one who can legally use it as a Facebook profile picture!

As I sat there, grinning out at the audience, I remembered the moment when I told people that I was entering Miss England and they could barely contain their laughter. Ha! I thought. Who would dare now to say that a girl in the Army couldn't take part in a beauty competition and win? I had rewritten the rulebook, surprising as it was that this had meant learning how to clean a rifle and how to walk correctly on a catwalk.

But for those first few weeks my biggest problem wasn't

walking in high heels, but simply getting across the country. I was lucky enough to be invited to be an ambassador for Vauxhall as part of my prize for being Miss England; they even threw in a free car for me to use for the year. The trouble was, the roads were covered in ice so it was a while before I could really get going.

But the roads cleared in the end and so I was able to properly begin my role as Miss England. One of the main tasks is to judge the regional heats for the next year's competition. It's a little bit sad that such a big part of your role should be to help find the person who is going to replace you; it does keep you grounded, though, as you're constantly reminded this isn't forever. To organise when and where I needed to be, every couple of weeks, I would head up to the Miss England offices in Leicester for a catch-up with Angie.

You would never know they are the Miss England offices from the outside – the building just looks like another house on an ordinary street – but you're not inside for long before you realise that you truly have entered the Kingdom of Miss England. Everything seems calm, beige, smart and glamorous... then you turn a corner and realise that at the end of the corridor you are walking down is the Miss England throne, twinkling away. And as you continue down that corridor you'll see that the walls are covered with enormous photographs of the winners, past and present. It really is a very special place and I love going there.

Once you are Miss England, Angie acts as part manager,

part agent and part showbiz agony aunt. In the 1980s, she was a major face on the beauty pageant scene when she won 85 pageants. She looks just like Sandra Bullock in *Miss Congeniality* and there's barely anything about the pageant world that can shock her; she has seen it all before and knows how to spot a nasty piece of work from quite a distance. That's what has made working with her such a treat – you might be sitting at a desk next to a throne, but your meeting is with one of the most down-to-earth people in the business.

Another part of the role is the charity work that you are invited to do. It is by no means compulsory, but it's a big part of the reason why I became involved in Miss England, so I always try to do as much as I can, from attending events as the face of the Royal British Legion or Help for Heroes to simply doing press to raise awareness of the charities and events that the Miss World organisation has on.

These activities have meant that I spent a huge part of 2010 racing up and down the country in my car. I never would have imagined there would be so much to see and so many differences in all the areas. I've really enjoyed travelling around, meeting all the girls and finding out why they want to be the next Miss England; I've also visited places that I never would have done otherwise, and this has not only opened my eyes to other cultures, but made me see what a great country we are and how much we have to offer. Serving in the Armed Forces instils a deep and lasting sense of pride in you and these experiences have served to emphasise that.

Another opportunity I had during my time as Miss England was to be the face of Uniform Dating, a dating website for people in uniform. This doesn't just mean those in the Forces, but firemen, nurses, prison workers and anyone who wears uniform for work or is interested in meeting them. I know what you're thinking, as it's exactly what I thought when they first approached me: kinky! But it's not really about the uniforms at all: it's a community of people who understand what it's like to work strange shift patterns, to be separated from their loved ones for months on end or to have a job that demands such a strong sense of loyalty to your chosen profession. All of these workers have selected their job as a way of life, not just a way to earn money, and it helps to be in a relationship with someone who understands that. If you're not interested in an ordinary desk job, then you may well want to meet others with the same sort of drive as you.

The work I have done for them is to help promote the site and to do an agony aunt column for them, as well as blogs and YouTube videos. I often get questions about dating, which I always try to do my best with and I'm always empathetic to those who are worried about keeping long-term relationships going while one or both of you is sent on exercise or to tour abroad for months on end. I met my partner Neil through the Army, in Iraq in 2005, and I'm always glad to be with someone who is also in the

Forces – he understands the way of life and how difficult the separation and shift patterns can be.

As with the Army, much about my time as Miss England has not been how I expected it to be; more importantly, it hasn't been what other people expected it to be either. The perception seems to be that once you are crowned Miss England, you immediately begin a life of being transported around the country in a fairy princess carriage not unlike the one that Katie Price arrived in for her wedding to Peter Andre. You don't change, but the people around you can alter; often they seem to believe that you are instantly hugely wealthy, which simply isn't the case. Yes, you get paid for appearances at Miss England heats, but it isn't a fortune. Depending on the amount of charity work that the winners take on, several of them choose to keep their everyday jobs on, at least part time.

My friend Laura who was Miss Ireland, for instance, has worked part-time at Tesco for years, with a tight-knit group of friends and a real sense of security there. She enjoys her work and decided to stay on part-time while fulfilling her role as Miss Ireland, but the *Daily Mail* took some photographs of her coming out of the supermarket and ran a very cruel story, implying that things somehow hadn't worked out for her, or she had made a massive mess of her life. No one ever thought to ask if it had been her decision to stay on there, or to suggest it might be a good thing that she had. Laura is just an honest, humble girl, who enjoys the company of her co-workers at the store and the sense of hard work and structure that the job gives her.

I don't blame Laura for keeping her job on, as there have certainly been times when I have felt a little lonely as Miss England – it being a unique role, even slightly surreal. Sometimes I have been at amazingly glamorous events such as Royal Ascot Ladies Day and been modelling for a company; I've had access to the Royal Enclosure and more celebrities and nobility than you could shake a stick at, while sipping eye-wateringly expensive champagne, but it has occasionally made me feel a little sad to be there without a friend or boyfriend to giggle at it all. Occasionally I've driven nine hours somewhere, arrived exhausted and dreaming of a pizza in my pyjamas in front of a good bit of telly, but had to spend a few hours chatting to strangers, while wearing a stiff frock and a face full of make-up.

It's difficult feeling that you can't ever have an 'off' day. I chose to put myself out there as Miss England so I have always accepted that I must represent the country and the organisation as best as I possibly can. If your 'product' is your personality, then you really can't turn that off. The only element I have genuinely struggled with is the press's interest in my private life. Ever since I began competing in Miss England, I have had a long-term boyfriend and I have never on any occasion discussed him in the media. This is partly because I feel there are some aspects of your life that you simply cannot make available for 'public consumption' and partly because Neil is also in the Army, and there would be security implications in his name and the specifics of his job being made public. Needless to say, there's nothing that I would ever do that might put his life or welfare at risk, or that of his colleagues.

Amid the dazzle the biggest dream of all has been a personal one: Neil and I became engaged in 2008, and once my time competing as Miss England had come to an end in 2009, we decided to plan our wedding. We always knew that we wanted to get married abroad and planned our dream ceremony on the beach in Sri Lanka for summer 2010. As ever, I didn't want to do things the traditional way and Neil completely agreed. There were to be only 20 guests, our closest friends and family, and as I was supposed to have been back at my Army job by then, there would have been no public interest in it at all.

When Rachel Christie was suddenly dethroned and I became Miss England, I decided to look into cancelling or at least postponing the wedding – I wasn't sure if 'Miss' England was actually allowed to be a 'Mrs'! It would have been hugely expensive for our friends and family who had saved up for it though, which meant cancelling would have been incredibly selfish. So Neil and I decided to go ahead with the ceremony and asked everyone to keep the event top secret until I was no longer Miss England. Everything went as planned and we had the wedding of our dreams, but then the week of Miss England 2010, I found out that the *Sun* had got details of the event. As only the few of us who were there that day knew about it, I realised that someone close to me had sold the story. To this day, I don't know who it was.

I was driving home one afternoon when Neil called and just said: 'Don't come home – there are hundreds of press outside of the house.' There were *Sky News* cameras, paparazzi, nosy bystanders, the lot – I didn't want to face them as I didn't want to be rude to them. I never had any intention of giving interviews about my private life, but I didn't want them to get footage of me refusing to talk either as I knew this could be interpreted as me being sulky or uncooperative. If we had done magazine shoots together or tweeted photographs of our home it would be very different and the press would have been entitled to be interested, but I'm not the kind of person who does that or ever will. No one will tell me how to conduct my relationships, thank you very much!

There was only one thing for it: I couldn't go back to the house. Luckily no one knows what Neil looks like and so he was able to pack some clothes for me and meet me in a nearby park in a different car. Within a couple of days, the new Miss England had been crowned and interest had moved on, but it's one side of my time as Miss England that I was not sad to say goodbye to.

It was a short-term inconvenience, though and not making a fuss about it helped the story to die down. Overall, being Miss England has been a dream come true: there are greater hardships than wearing slightly uncomfortable shoes for a few hours, as I frequently remind myself whenever I talk to my Army friends. Fighting for the country, literally risking your life for it, is considerably harder work than smiling for it at a charity function – and most of them are great fun.

I have often been asked what the highlight of my year as Miss England was and I can honestly say that it was every single day, as they have all been so different. I've been interviewed by magazines such as *Hello, OK!, Closer* and even had a double page spread in *FHM*, and I've been on Radio 1, the Jeremy Vine's Radio 2 s Show and appeared on Frank Skinner's *Opinionated* TV comedy show to discuss beauty. I have also loved my appearances on *GMTV*, although the most fun I ever had at an interview was at Rock FM, where I had to paintball the DJ's crotch for ages while listeners called in with questions – it was quite a change of scene from Army days!

There have been days when I've been up at 5am, standing in a dress made of lottery balls for a shoot for the National Lottery, others when I've found myself chatting to Barbara Windsor and Lulu at a Variety Club ball and still more when I've woken up surrounded in luxury at international events. The most glamorous event that I attended was definitely the Miss Gibraltar competition, where I was invited as a judge. Kaiane, the current Miss World, was Miss Gibraltar and she was one of the girls that I got on best with in South Africa, so it was a real treat for me to catch up with her. What I wasn't prepared for, however, was the level of intense glitz and glamour that the competition would involve.

Only ten finalists are selected, so the competition itself was relatively small, but the show that they put on was nothing short of spectacular. It was a Las Vegas-standard event, with fireworks, dancers and what must have been months' worth of rehearsals and preparations. When Kaiane appeared on stage, the audience went crazy; the atmosphere was electric. It certainly helped that I was fully rested for the occasion, as I was staying in a stunning hotel with a rooftop swimming pool, a bottle of champagne in my room and full VIP treatment. It was one of those moments you look forward to telling your family and friends about.

No matter how extravagant or dazzling some of the events I have attended have been, there has been one element of my year as Miss England that has meant the most to me: my time with the competitors for this year. Without doubt, nurturing them and working on their confidence has been the most important task I have carried out.

I have done my best to be a sympathetic judge as I remember how nervous I myself was such a short time ago: I feel very strongly that young girls should be doing events that build their self-esteem and do not knock it, and I believe that Miss England can be one of them. A lot of people have an unpleasant, inflexible idea of what a beauty queen is and I'm not going to lie about the fact that I did, too until a couple of years ago when I started to find out for myself.

I quickly realised that the girls who enter the competition are often the most intelligent and warm-hearted women you could wish to meet. I'm so thankful to have met so many lovely new friends through my involvement in the organisation. We have become a real little family! As a result, I have worked hard to try and change the stereotype of what the Miss England competition actually is. Through the course of the year, I noticed again and again that if there is ever any reference to pageants in the media, it is always illustrated with dated old images of 'bathing beauties' parading around in bikinis. Why did everyone still think that the competition was about who looks the best in a swimsuit? When would they realise that it was so much more than that? I was getting fed up with it, especially as the bikini round had always been my worst by a considerable margin.

The next time that I went to the Miss England offices I suggested removing the swimsuit round altogether might make people sit up and take notice of the fact that it is no longer just about having the best bikini body. Surely getting rid of it once and for all would help girls' confidence while also helping to promote the other things that beauty queens do, such as all the amazing charity work? Beauty is about so much more than looks and it is worth very little without confidence!

I am proud to say that the swimwear round has now been removed. This wasn't just a victory for me, but for all the girls who feel, mistakenly, that what you look like in a bikini is the only valid way you can be judged. The decision was reported worldwide and I hope that young women out there have taken heart from it. We decided to replace it with a sports round instead; this means that the emphasis is now on health rather than a dated idea of beauty. These days, obesity is a bigger problem than anorexia, so shifting the emphasis to fitness sends a message that young women should appreciate their bodies for being strong and healthy rather than just bulge-free.

The year 2010 was the first one for 24 years when Miss England was shown on TV again and I'm sure that it's because without the bikini round it feels like less of a criticism of what women can be and more of a celebration. I want Miss England to be a place where girliness and an appreciation of femininity can be expressed without having to be that kind of cartoonish stereotype of womanliness. It's about being an ambassador for what women can achieve, not about looking good in a bikini. If nothing else, I hope this is one legacy I will leave as Miss England: I don't want to be remembered as having discovered the best way to make hair extensions look good after a three-hour train ride, but for having made some otherwise anxious young girls feel good about themselves.

I never set out to be a role model but now I can see that I am, I make the most of it and hope that I encourage others to go for it and surprise themselves with their achievements, too. In both the Army and the pageant world, I thought that I was going to be negatively judged for not being the 'right kind' of person but what I learned was that because I simply joined in and gave it my all wherever I was, I have had nothing but support from both areas. I take my hair and make-up seriously, and I take my work for the military seriously: it is possible to do both.

I do feel that I have made a difference as I am often emailed or receive Facebook messages from women telling me that I have changed perceptions, that they would never have dared to enter the contest if the swimwear round was still a part of it, or that they now have the courage to join the Army because they have seen that someone as feminine as me is a serving soldier.

So many women mistakenly think that life in the Army is nothing more than rolling around in the mud, or struggling to fit in an exclusively masculine world. They thought that they would be laughed at for trying; nothing could be further from the truth.

I have even managed to convince some of the Miss England competitors to join up! Last time I saw Miss Colchester, she had just taken her BARB test and was about to begin training. Women can do anything if they put their minds to it and to have convinced a few of them that that is the case makes me proud.

My time as Miss England was never going to last forever, even though they did extend it from July to September, to make up for the time that Rachel Christie had had the crown. But in September the Miss England 2010 competition suddenly came rolling round and it was time to hand over the title.

I was told by the Miss England officials that all I needed to do was to turn up, look glamorous and hand over the crown, but I wanted to make sure that I both did them proud and savoured every moment instead of lying around at home until the last minute. After all, I had become very fond of a lot of the girls as a result of competing with them in previous years and then being a regional judge all year.

Over the course of the year I had been met with almost nothing but friendliness and enthusiasm. Only once or twice were there crazy 'Pageant Mums' who came and screamed in my face if their precious daughter didn't win. On the whole, it was an empowering experience, proving again and again that getting your hair 'just so' will never be as important as showing a little bit of kindness and respect to your fellow competitors.

I decided to dress casually for the two days of preparation before the big event. On the first day, I turned up in a jumpsuit and then on the second day, I wore simple black leggings and an official Miss England jumper, which has the emblem on the front in crystals. I took with me the same book that I had had at Miss World and asked all of the girls to sign it – I wanted it to eventually be filled with all of the Miss World and Miss England competitors. Taking it around to the girls during rehearsals was a really emotional moment for all of us. I was so excited about handing over the title to one of them, but at the same time sad that this important chapter in my life was coming to an end.

I watched the talent round and the eco round with interest, remembering all of my own experiences as I did so. Miss Sunderland won the talent round as she had a truly beautiful singing voice and the eco round – which had no theme at all this time – was won by Siobhan Brindley, who was deaf. She had created an incredible outfit: a full carnival costume made entirely from bits of trash. It could easily have been worn in Rio or Trinidad – and luckily for her, she could also sit and move in it!

Finally, after the two days of preparation and rehearsals, the moment of the final gala arrived. It was held at the Birmingham Hilton Metropole: the stage was enormous, there was a huge crew and seven members of the Army, who I had arranged to come and escort the girls, on and offstage.

At half time I went backstage myself, while they showed a video about my time as Miss England. It made a huge well of emotions bubble up inside of me, but I was determined not to start crying and ruin such a moment of celebration. Next, I walked slowly up onto the stage, through the audience, as the speakers played Whitney Houston's 'One Moment In Time'. As I approached the throne, which was by now centre stage, everyone in the audience started to stand and clap. I could see the friends I had made in floods of tears while my dad and Neil were in the audience, welling up. Still, I just about managed to keep it together.

Next, all of the finalists came up on stage and it was my

role to call out the top twenty girls. I knew so many of them, it was weird to be calling out their names and then going through their interview on stage, while secretly thinking, oh, I so hope you do well – you're a credit to the competition. To me, it was so important that I would pass on my crown to someone who would respect all of the work I had done: I had put so much time and effort into changing the perception of Miss England, I didn't want to simply hand over the reins to someone who might come along and put it all to waste.

The excitement of the moment began to catch up with me as I looked around the stage, feeling increasingly nervous, thinking, is it going to be you? Or you? Oh, I hope it's you... or actually you. As the emotions bubbled ever higher, I went to stand by the throne for the very last time.

In a way, I was starting to feel a little bit lost: I had never thought that Miss England would become such an important part of my life, but then it did. I found myself standing there under the stage lights, thinking: what's going to happen next? What could possibly come after this? On the other hand, I was prouder than ever before – not only had I become Miss England but I'd done it on my own terms and genuinely changed things for the next group of girls.

I was determined not to shed a tear: not just because I wanted to celebrate the new Miss England, but because I wanted to make sure that no one thought I was crying because I didn't want to hand over. No one likes a desperate old beauty queen hanging onto the crown for dear life!

The momentary blur cleared and I heard the compère announce who was in third place. Next, he announced the runner up, who was a good friend of mine. As she came to take her place on the stage, I gave her such a huge hug that I nearly lifted her clean off the stage! Then, there was a pause. As if I was a competitor all over again, I found myself staring at the judges and trying to guess what they had been thinking. Who would it be?

Finally, the compère announced that Miss England 2010 was Miss Nottingham: Jessica Linley. I had first met Jess over two years ago on the first day that I had ever met any Miss England girls, when I had travelled to London to model the Miss England bikinis on the King's Road. She had become a good friend and stayed so loyal to me throughout my crazy year. I could not have been more thrilled by her being the winner: she is stunningly beautiful, blonde with blue eyes, as if she is devoted to nothing more in life than looking good. People often assume that she's nothing more than a ditsy blonde but she has just qualified as a lawyer, which always shocks them. It means a lot to me that she is both a nice girl and a smart girl. I have never worried that she will ever do anything to do down the image of Miss England, but will continue to develop it for the future.

Once Jess's name was called, she walked to the front of

the stage and sat on the Miss England throne. I walked up to stand behind her and took the crown from my head. I know it's cheesy, but as I took it off, I gave it a kiss goodbye, waved at it and then the audience, and finally placed it upon her head. Next, I presented her with the sash and gave her a kiss to say congratulations.

Almost immediately I went from feeling sad that this part of my life was over to feeling happy that Jess was now Miss England. But before I had a chance to dwell on my own feelings any more, there was a sudden explosion of glitter and camera flashes and the audience went wild with applause for the new Miss England.

I stepped to one side of the stage to let Jess enjoy her moment of glory and savoured the fact that for the first time in a year, I was doing the watching for once instead of being centre stage; it was only after the event that people mentioned to me that I wasn't in any of the photographs.

'Where did you go?' they asked. I suppose instinct told me it really was time to hand over my time in the spotlight and when the moment came, I did it with surprising ease. I don't cherish fame for fame's sake and have turned down a lot of interest and opportunities, such as *Celebrity Big Brother* and *I'm a Celebrity... Get Me Out Of Here!* to concentrate on the kind of work that I think I'm best at. There is no point in having any profile unless you are doing something useful with it, and I suppose it might take me a while to reconcile the two in a new way.

In the short term, I headed back to my Army role within

a fortnight of Miss England 2010, looking forward to returning to a bit of routine. I missed my job, but I was apprehensive about going back as I knew that there would be an element of having to prove myself again. I don't just want to be known on the barracks as the girl who swanned off to become Miss England. The difference is, this time I know I can do it, as I have proved to myself and others that I don't have to live up to anyone's else's expectations of me.

What next for Combat Barbie? It is hard to say as this has already been an incredible journey for a girl who could barely walk in high heels a couple of years ago, and not so long before had barely a clue as to what she could do with her life. It's amazing how quickly life can change based on just a few decisions: when I look back, it was only my own nervousness and insecurity that was stopping me from doing any of this sooner. I proved that I was good enough for the Army, and I proved that I was good enough for Miss England – and I did it on my own terms.

It's not what I do next that is important to me: it's *how* I do it. I have a core of people around me, who love me and mean the world to me, so it's maintaining those relationships that gives me the strength to do everything else my own way – and so can everyone else.